The Perils of

Being a House Guest

The Pitfalls of
Being a House Guest

MATTHEW LAZENBY

Published by Bouverie Press

A CIP catalogue record for this book is available from the British Library.

ISBN 978-1-7384885-0-6

Book layout and cover design by Clare Brayshaw
Illustration 128346034 | Abstract © Egor Suvorov | Dreamstime.com

Prepared and printed by:

York Publishing Services Ltd
64 Hallfield Road
Layerthorpe
York YO31 7ZQ

Tel: 01904 431213

Website: www.yps-publishing.co.uk

Contents

Foreword

Whether you are visiting your second cousin in Sorrento or taking refuge on a friend's sofa after a vicious game of Scrabble has caused you to miss the last train back to Huddersfield, a night staying in someone else's home can be a minefield of misadventure.

Whatever the circumstances that may have led up to a stay on someone's spare bed or settee, or the nature of the relationship between you and your host, there is no denying that being a guest in someone's home – welcome or otherwise – deepens your bond with them. To be invited to spend the night in someone's house is a sign that the person feels comfortable opening up their sanctuary to you. They want – or begrudgingly accept – you in their life and are happy for you to see the most authentic version of themselves. They might even run the risk of letting you see them without make-up. At the very least, for someone to have made space for you merely as a practical gesture is an affirmation of personal approval because they presumably wouldn't have entertained the idea of hosting you if they thought you were a loutish ruffian. Still, taking up temporary residence in the inner sanctum of someone else's existence can leave one susceptible to an astonishing and dazzling array of potential pitfalls and faux pas.

Unfolding shortly is a chronological commentary on the perils that can often greet the unsuspecting house guest. I have encountered a great many of these hazards first-hand and have heard about countless more from other survivors.

Professionally, I am that most idiosyncratic species: a church organist. I am frequently to be found giving concerts and conducting choirs in obscure corners of the British Isles and in France, an existence which takes me around a lot of spare bedrooms, a lot of sofas and over a lot of creaky floorboards in the middle of the night. I am penning this volume after years of attempting, not always successfully, to show my appreciation for people's kindly offers of accommodation via such gestures as not damaging their pets or not causing their houses to catch fire. I must put on the record that am profoundly grateful to all who are sufficiently generous and brave as to allow me into their homes. However, all this fine hospitality has given me an acute awareness of just what a dangerous business being a house guest can be.

This book is perhaps more reflective than advisory. I don't pretend to have all the solutions. Indeed, one might surmise in due course that I am scarcely a safe bet to be set free beyond my own front door without close supervision. After all, it is years of coming adrift and making a well-intentioned arse of myself in my capacity as a guest that has inspired me to share my cautionary tales. There are many hurdles to jump, many tightropes of etiquette to tread and many potential dropped balls that could see both guest and host scarred for life, or at least until morning. Let us now imagine that night has fallen and you are about to be left to your own devices for a night of repose on unchartered territory. It promises to be a wild ride.

ONE

Pre-Bedtime Talk with Host

Your having spent a convivial evening with your host, or alternatively having turned up on their doorstep at an hour so late that they opened the door bleary-eyed and inadequately feigned being pleased to see you, the time eventually comes for everyone to retire to bed. This is where the robustly happy-go-lucky daytime dynamic between you and your host can start to take on a more mysterious and delicate character.

The arrival of bedtime is often your first opportunity to read between the lines and demonstrate an advanced level of social intuition. Usually, in my experience, the conversation reaches a contentedly drowsy lull, at which point your host might betray a telling yawn to signal either that they are tired or that you have talked for slightly too long about the adrenalin highlights of the previous weekend's quilt show. The yawn having served as evidence of their fatigue, they then say something along the lines of 'Well I don't know about you, but I think I'd better get some sleep,' almost guiltily, even though you were actually waiting for the cue and could well have been for some hours. This is a not-altogether-subtle hint that, regardless of your state of tiredness, it is Closing Time as far as downstairs is concerned – unless staying in a bungalow or apartment, of course – and that it is time to adjourn to separate quarters and suspend acquaintance until the next morning. However much the host may make it sound like you are under no pressure to follow suit, I've never been sure whether it's the done thing to say 'OK, sleep well,' and then remain in the living room banging out rousing ragtime classics on the piano for another hour. Probably not.

Once the day is unanimously carried as having ended, there follows a brief guest information presentation from your host outlining night-time practicalities and the morning regime. In this digital age, the first thing people often tell you, in some cases taking precedence over such comparative minutiae as the location of the bathroom, is the Wi-Fi password.

What an eccentric ritual this has become. Every activity that includes being in situ for more than five minutes, be it sitting down in a coffee shop, going on a train or making first acquaintance with a hotel room, to name but three examples, is now routinely prefaced with the rite of preparation that is urgently finding Wi-Fi access. Once the network has been identified, everyone in the party must then anxiously wait for their device to plumb them into an acute awareness of absolutely everything going on in the world except the activity in the present for which they have assembled friends and paid money. Only when we're hooked up to an intravenous drip of the virtual are we able to feel at ease with the real, or so it seems. It's like Wi-Fi is a kind of oxygen. It is an insurance policy against boredom and an escape lane for the mind.

I have never seen such disproportionate agitation as when my friend brought his teenage sons along on a visit to a famous medieval cathedral and I had to break the news to them that, despite or perhaps thanks to the presence of the Holy Spirit, there was no public Wi-Fi offered on the premises. Visible discomfort, induced by a sudden digital disconnect, had already struck the adolescents while walking between the Wi-Fi-enabled café and the cathedral door. The teens were disturbingly devastated when I broke the news of the sacred building's technological shortcomings. This could not just have been a recent complaint; presumably, the central tower had been erected to its two-hundred-and-thirty-five-foot loftiness so that fifteenth-century worshippers could hot-foot to the top and profit from an unrivalled 4G signal to assist with the live streaming of services online or to download a tasty recipe for gelyne-in-broth or perhaps some gyngerbrede. Anyway, any host now knows that the Wi-Fi password is the first thing anyone under eighty will require to function and feel comfortable in the home environment.

'Do you have everything you need?' your host might well ask. This question is often redundant – it's seldom appropriate to ask for a pedicure and you don't realise until you've parted company for the night that you've forgotten your toothbrush, by which time there's nothing you can do about it. Some hosts then cheerfully throw in something along the lines of 'Help yourself if you need anything from the kitchen'. I have never fully worked out how sincerely this is meant. It is a warm and generous invitation from which both sides profit. The host sleeps soundly in the knowledge that the bountifully stocked fridge will provide for any nutritional whim of the guest, thus emotionally insuring the host against any self-doubt about the generosity of their hospitality. The guest, meanwhile, can enjoy the theoretical luxury of wanting for nothing that cannot be found in the larder. This said, just how literally should one interpret this offer? I have never quite had the balls to conduct a social experiment in which my host retires to bed with the words 'Help yourself to anything from the kitchen' and I subsequently greet them the next morning with the words 'I'm afraid you're now out of ham'. I was particularly touched by the kindness of a friend with whom I stayed a couple of years ago. Even though he had to be up early the next morning for work, he would make a sandwich before bed and put it in a plastic box in the fridge along with some carrot sticks and an apple, presumably in case I got hungry during the night. Halfway through the week, this practice lapsed along with his sunny and benevolent temperament and I never quite figured out why.

Your host's information presentation might then feature a plethora of additional domestic advice specific to the household: a cast list (or, indeed, a cat list) of the animals that could potentially enter your room in the night and how to respond to them, directions to additional layers of bedding in the cupboards, hints and tips for getting to sleep on a folding bed without developing a musculoskeletal disorder, which of the many bathrooms is the optimal one to use and with whom you will be sharing the facility, any special instructions about the locking or whistling procedure associated with the bathroom door, the level of stealth and precision with which you must proceed in order not to set off the burglar alarm at 3 AM, or anything else of peculiarity to the premises.

The briefing typically concludes with a rundown of the morning's getting-up arrangements. This might constitute a baffling code of practice explaining who goes to work at what time, who needs the bathroom at what time and how long people like to spend studying the morning paper in strict isolation before they leave the house. If you have received such detailed particulars as these, it is usually as well to remain quarantined in your bedroom until at least midday just to be sure you're not interrupting anything. Alternatively, the nature of the advice might be the polar opposite, that you should 'just get up when you feel like it'. This latter possibility, as we will discuss later, is as disquietingly vague as the former is dauntingly detailed and will see you waking up at 5:30 AM and wondering what's expected of you.

A genial 'goodnight' and that's it. You're now on your own until morning. Your host might jauntily have said 'Give me a shout if you need anything' but this isn't really something you should pursue unless the place is on fire, particularly if said host is not sleeping alone. Your challenge now is to conduct yourself in a discreet and respectable fashion for the next eight or nine hours. You must perform all bathroom routines and get a good night's sleep while taking care not to damage the house, wake anyone from slumber or generally make a nuisance of yourself. Having deftly navigated your way through the hours of darkness, you will subsequently present yourself brightly and cheerfully to your host in the morning. You will be radiating joy because you slept like the proverbial log and your host will be feeling suitably ebullient because, in addition to their having the pleasure of your company at the breakfast table, you didn't wake them up at 4 AM by tripping over the dog and demolishing their favourite vase en route to the lavatory. How hard can it be?

TWO

Entering the Bedroom

Shortly after you and your host have parted ways for the night, you will most likely enter your bedroom or other designated night-time space. Once alone in your sleeping room, you will set about attempting to make it the most comfortable and ergonomically friendly nest possible for the night. You might initially close the curtains or their equivalent – a minefield so complex as to merit its own chapters – and then go about getting yourself fully installed in the room.

One of your first decisions might be which side of a double bed you are going to occupy. Your choice might be influenced by the location of a vacant plug socket, especially if you are relying on your phone's alarm to activate your morning consciousness. Alarm clocks, along with cameras, calculators and torches, have become another item of monofunctional apparatus to be made obsolete by our mobile phones, which must now be charged overnight at the bedside in order to wake us in a timely fashion. Indeed, we expect them to do this by playing our preferred music the number of times we desire and vibrating in whatever way optimises our pleasure. I always feel thoroughly apprehensive if there is no bedside phone-charging facility and I am embarrassed to admit that such an omission throws me onto the horns of a serious dilemma. If my phone has to be fuelled on the other side of the room, I may not hear its attempts to summon me in the morning. On the other hand, if I leave it on my bedside unplugged, I fear that the battery could well expire before the alarm is due, even if the phone is one hundred per cent charged before I go to sleep. Such reckless gambling with the next morning's prospects is not the basis for a good night's repose. It is the same neurotic state of mind that can make us write down uncompleted tasks that we suddenly remember and worry about upon getting into bed, fearing that our memories will restore factory settings overnight, wipe themselves clean and ensure that said tasks remain unfulfilled.

Some may condemn my wailing about not being able to recharge my phone overnight as a symptom of the feckless millennial hyper-dependence on these devices but the same people might also express contempt if they were anticipating a morning appointment with a millennial who had failed to be aroused from slumber. Your bedside table might quaintly be equipped with an alarm clock but I think many of us are as likely to succeed in setting an unknown and venerable mains-powered radio alarm contraption at bedtime as we are to reap success in setting the clock of a new oven or car without having first attained a diploma in electronic engineering. We are similarly unlikely to be arsed with the challenge. If I were to partake in an intellectual contest at bedtime with a thirty-year-old digital alarm clock as my opponent, it would probably take until sunrise for me to work out how to instruct the thing to do anything more useful than manically flashing the time in Uganda or reciting the shipping forecast.

After weighing up the risks associated with night-time phone charging, hopefully having not lost too large a percentage of the night's available sleeping time in doing so, your next move is to plug the charger in. It is astonishing how much noise can be generated by a plug entering its socket after nightfall. This is particularly the case in modern houses with thin walls. If you plug something in after the household has settled down for the night in such a dwelling, those sleeping elsewhere in the house might be awoken by a sound not unlike someone penetrating the wall with a hammer and chisel. Equally, you might be awoken by this daunting sound when someone else connects their hardware to the mains in a different part of the house. If they do this on an adjoining wall, you will be momentarily unsettled by the possibility that they are trying to infiltrate your sanctuary via the aid of a pickaxe. By day, of course, the plugging in of our contraptions is a completely mundane and silent operation.

A towel will often await you on the end of the bed, sometimes two or three, and if there are two or three I'm never quite sure what I'm supposed to do with them all. It's almost like multiple sets of cutlery laid out for the same person for the same meal. Being worldly and enlightened, I am aware that the latter is not because I'm anticipated to be such a clumsy fool as to drop my knife and fork on the floor repeatedly while eating. However, I don't yet know what I'm supposed to do with a multitude of towels over the course of a one-night stay. In the past, I have been known to use one of them as a make-shift window hanging when I've been defeated by the modus operandi of the blind, but this was probably not what my hosts had in mind. Indeed, I have occasionally received text messages confirming my misuse of the towels when I've forgotten to remove my improvised window coverings before departure.

As mentioned earlier, your host may well have given you a Wi-Fi password. Since this is vital for deep and restorative sleep, you might now spend a diverting twenty minutes attempting to decipher it. Many years ago, my friend asked her elderly father, who was beset with declining eyesight, to read out his credit card number over the phone to her so that she could order something online on his behalf. My friend asked him to read the number back several times and each attempt produced a subtly different order of numbers from the last. In the end, since the sun had set in its entirety during this challenged exchange, my friend submitted an average of all the potential sixteen-digit numbers with which she'd been supplied and, amazingly, got it right. Back in the guest room, you might now be puzzling over a disorderly and non-uniform string of handwritten characters on a scrap of paper and, if you are sufficiently intelligent and applied as to crack the code, your reward will be not having to use your own network data to scroll through stimulating digital content before going to sleep. Is the fourth character a '1,' an 'l,' an 'I' or a '7'? Is the sixth character an uppercase 'S' or lower? Is it in fact a '5'? Perhaps the first 'O' was indeed an 'O' but the second one is an '0'. Did your host make an error with the third 'O' and therefore cross it out or are you in fact in Norway? Maybe there isn't a full stop in the line-up at all but a passing ant decided to take a crafty plop on the paper while you were scratching your head in asemic befuddlement.

Before the graphological challenge, you will of course have had to find the network from a list. Sometimes these lists of available networks, especially in apartment buildings with a high density of networks from which to choose, burst at the seams with cutting-edge wit. I was particularly pleased for my friend on his choice of fiancée when I discovered that theirs was 'Wi Believe I can Fi,' as christened by the lady of the house. The network you're wanting will doubtlessly be the one that only shows up some of the time, usually for half an hour somewhere between nine and eleven in the morning. Larger dwellings might have an assortment of networks to join depending on which wing of the property you're in. By the time you have succeeded in connecting, you will decide that none of the things you might have wished to do on your phone at the beginning of the process could compare with the rapturous contentment of abandoning your device and going to sleep.

Having navigated all this cybernetic chicanery, it is sensible to identify a prominent surface on which you might place together all your more losable items, such as your watch, jewellery and so forth. An ideal spot might be the bedside table, on which might also rest your phone if you've opted to keep it close by. But bedside tables can get very busy. They typically offer a lamp, which your host might have left switched on to create a vibe of calm visibility. This calmness might turn to mild rage when you try to switch the lamp off, as you attempt to locate the switch and burn your hand on the bulb before realising you're supposed to tap on the base with a secret combination of knuckles, the cycle of brightness settings transforming the room into a small lighthouse before darkness can be attained.

Vying for space next to the lamp might be the aforementioned alarm clock, whose misleading temporal assertions might remind you of the importance of not taking things at 'face value'. There might also be some tissues, perhaps a small but priceless vase for you to knock onto the floor while attempting to deactivate your morning alarm, and maybe a thoughtfully provided glass of water. I don't typically make it through to morning without treating myself and my surroundings to an inadvertent dousing with the latter, which has been known to follow gamely behind the vase in its urgent rush to the hard floor courtesy of my drowsily off-target efforts to stab the alarm to silence.

Bedside tables come in a variety of guises. In a guest room, the bedside furniture could be pretty much anything that has either been improvised for the purpose or secreted in there in the name of getting a redundant or unfashionable item of furniture out of the homeowner's daily sightline. It could be a small stool – hopefully of the type you're supposed to sit on. It could alternatively be an aged and garishly decorated cabinet that has been kept in the family for sentimental reasons. It could merely be a precarious pile of books or, in a more left-field household, it could be something that your host is trying to pass off as an exceptionally hipster or alternative design statement. The 'coolest' thing I ever came across playing this rôle was to be found in the bachelor pad of an alpha male who had identified the height and flat top of a stocked mini-fridge as meeting the criteria for a bedside shelf. It was a huge novelty to be able to reach for a chilled beer or a bottle of milk at three in the morning without alighting from the bed. This was also the approximate time that the loud and unrelenting hum that had serenaded me for four conscious hours was joined by the soothing gurgling of the contraption's defrosting regime. I thought it funny that my host hadn't repeated this masterstroke of creativity and convenience in his own bedroom.

At the other end of the spectrum, I recently stayed with an interior designer with a hip and minimalist spare room which boasted exceedingly sleek tables on either side of the bed, designed specifically for the service they were providing. Regrettably, they were made of thin metal and were highly resonant. Every time I placed anything down on one it sounded like I was banging a large gong. They were evidently not unique to my room: the rest of the house intermittently reverberated to the same percussive sound throughout the night when people were inspired to place things down on their tables in the early hours. If these tables had been available in different sizes and therefore different pitches, they could have served as low-cost alternatives to kettledrums. There could be some mileage in the commissioning of a piece of music for Bedside Table Orchestra, perhaps to be premiered in the Leeds branch of IKEA sometime in the autumn.

THREE

Curtains

The first thing you will probably do on entering your sleeping room is close the curtains. Ideally, you will have the presence of mind to do this before getting undressed because the phenomenon of stripping off and then realising that one has just provided after-dinner entertainment for the gentleman over the road can make one feel somewhat cheap. Moreover, it can provoke unnecessary questions and dangle a question mark over your previous good character. Neighbours' children might innocently comment during your inevitable coincidence in the street the next day that you look different with clothes on.

A lit room with open curtains is like a theatre for passers-by and there is an acute helplessness about your naked form winding up centre stage. Your fight-or-flight instincts dictate that the obvious recovery strategy is to close the curtains or blinds with a blunt urgency in order to shield yourself as quickly as possible. This prompts you to run uninhibited up to the window and briefly exhibit yourself in even greater detail, perhaps with slapstick over-animation. It is as if you are trying to bring value for money to the people in the cheap seats. You are betrayed by your instincts.

An alternative course of action could be to drop to the floor behind the bed in the manner of an ambushed soldier. This is all very well if your clothes are nearby and you can hide behind the bed to put them on. If they're not, you might now shuffle stealthily to the window in a seal-like manner to try closing the curtains, although your subsequent attempts to reach them could still see you advertising your wares to the neighbourhood.

If you are of a more rational disposition, you might simply think to switch the light back off instead. Indeed, doing this will almost certainly constitute the clever idea you think of afterwards if you have pursued one of the other options. At the other extreme, if the aforementioned fight-or-flight impulses are truly desperate to put an end to you, you might panic and run out of the room. This will almost certainly coincide with your host crossing the landing.

There's a good chance that your sleeping room will sport the traditional setup of a pair of curtains that you pull together in a few seconds before proceeding to get on with your life. However, a combination of aesthetic preferences, ease of fitting and operation, levels of darkness required and goodness knows what else means that making your bedroom opaque to the world can be a more complex and involved scenario in the twenty-first century than it might once have been.

If you find curtains in your bedroom, you will instinctively pull them together. If they obligingly close like curtains of the old school, all is well. However, they might resist and, if they do, it is sensible to check that they're not hooked up to some pseudo-labour-saving mechanism where one is to pull a cord at one end and then marvel as the curtains smoothly close, meeting in the middle in perfect symmetry. In reality, there is every chance of there being a large resultant gap in the middle despite the string refusing to be tugged any further. If you try to finish it off by hand, as it were, it will either have no effect at all or provoke a ripping sound or a terminal jolt as you corrupt the mechanism, possibly followed by a light glissando as you succeed, to your mild horror, in tearing the curtain from the rail.

More baffling still is when the curtains are electrified and operated via the push of a button. They slide together with an eerie whirring sound *à la crematorium*, but sometimes stop halfway and then start to emit smoke, as if the baddie is about to appear on stage at a pantomime. It is difficult to believe that these ideas were coined *after* the advent of the pullable curtain. There is a certain parallel with the coin-operated telescope. This was invented after many years of people using telescopes that worked perfectly well without the need to insert a two-pound coin to unlock the optical powers, although perhaps I have missed the point. In a similar vein, it is nominally interesting to note that the electric slow cooker was invented later than the microwave.

People sometimes have ornamental curtains. These are solely for decoration and not intended to be closed. Such curtains can usually be identified by a special effort having been made with their presentation. They might be tied back into an elegant position and many people would find it an inordinate faff to successfully recreate such a work of art each morning. For someone like me, such a consistently disciplined aesthetic endeavor would be almost laughably unattainable. These decorative curtains can often be rather translucent. If you suspect that the curtain at your window might fall into the 'ornamental' category, it is prudent to dig deeper for the item you're actually supposed to be using to block out the light. Hiding behind the frilly facade of the show curtains could well be something much more serviceable, such as a blind…

FOUR

Blinds

Blinds can be bewildering. They come in a variety of guises: roman, roller, venetian and vertical, to name but four. Each type is characterised by its own particular set of dysfunctional and exasperating traits. Some blinds are at war with themselves and it might appear that the parts of the blind that block out the light have voted for independence from both the mechanism and each other. Where this is the case, your tugging on the cord will correlate only very indirectly with the extent to which the window is covered. All you are doing by pulling is signalling to the blind that you wish it to unravel. How it does so is beyond your control. Alternatively, the blind's components may be in solid unity against a common enemy: you.

In the case of a roman blind, the bottom section of fabric will mischievously catch hold of a window handle or some such pesky obstacle early in its descent. The rest of the blind, however, will continue to unravel freely as you pull the cord. Forces eventually conspire to set free the stuck section, to which is usually attached a strip of heavy reinforcement made from a resistant material. This will then sacrifice itself downward with a startlingly gravitational plummet. Upon arriving at the bottom of the window, the blind will usually invade the personal space of a vase or photo frame, which will obligingly jump onto the floor beneath and shatter into a thousand pieces to free up space.

A vertical blind might offer an intimidating selection of cords from which to choose and they will all be intricately tangled together. One cord will make all but one of the blind slats twirl around as you stare at the window for a few seconds until you work out which variable you have activated, while one might collate the slats into a neatish assembly at one end of the window. A third cord might appear to do nothing at all but, as you continue to pull it and wear an expression of studious exasperation, you eventually observe – with a trill of mirth – that it has reopened the blinds of the next window along, those which you had just succeeded in closing. In any case, you will probably need to reattach at least three pieces of the setup before you can go to sleep.

A venetian blind might already be spread out across the window on your arrival but with the slats at the wrong angle for blocking out the light. Alternatively, the entire setup might be gathered tightly together and clinging to the top of the window. In any case, there will be a mysterious assortment of thin cords at one side, at least two of which will be joined together at the bottom by a piece of plastic. To lower the blind, you speculatively tug at the cords in turn, the first three of which will give aggressive resistance. The fourth one will lift up one side of the blind by a centimetre and then eject it down the window with startling gravity. The other side will remain firmly fixed to the top of the window, acting as a hinge as the blind unevenly spreads itself out like a folding fan. Instinctively, you will then heave the unravelled side back to the top, after which it will fix itself into place and inexplicably release the other side of the blind to perform the same stunt, hinged from the side that first came loose. Any attempt to keep the two sides at the same altitude and cover the entire window is rather like flying a kite in high winds as you jostle with the two strings and eventually vow to travel with an eye mask at all times.

It is said, although I am not sure where or by whom, that if you want to make a Venetian blind you should poke him in the eye. I once stayed in a house owned by someone who realised that a possible way of making *me* blind, or indeed unconscious, would be to perch a roller blind precariously between two brackets above the bedroom window, entirely unfixed to anything. Had I been a trespasser and not a guest, it would have been the perfect foil. The results were predictable. Failing to realise that this blind was merely in situ to portray the superficial impression of there being a window covering, lest the premises be perceived as low-spec, I naïvely pulled the cord and was comprehensively knocked to the floor by the weighty descent of the giant roll of canvas, my testicles and my head exchanging confused evening greetings on passing each other as the former jumped up in astonishment and the latter fell back somewhat numbly. My host came into the room to find me attempting to navigate my way out of the tent that had unravelled over me like an exceptionally shit human net-trap. The blind was subsequently rebalanced into position while I was cursed for breaking it. A hanging can of paint has probably been added to the setup by now, in anticipation of the next visitor.

It is very easy, of course, to forget to close the blinds altogether. If the room is already dark on entering and the window small, you might only register the need to close the blinds at 5 AM when the sun rises and sticks its middle finger up at you and your planned lie-in. Moreover, there are various other guises of blind and indeed many more potential blind-related exploits, the world of blinds being a justly popular sphere of discussion at dinner parties and a classic motif on which to enchant one's company on a first date. I have not yet mentioned the cordless blinds that one pulls down via a discreet plastic thing in the middle but which then teasingly ping straight back up when you let go, nor the so-called 'black-out' blinds that can have you thinking it's the middle of the night when it's actually three o'clock in the afternoon and you've missed the day. I could go on, but there is only so much trauma one can bear to relive.

FIVE

Shutters

If you are staying somewhere swanky or outside the UK – or both – your room might be kitted out with shutters. These are of course made of resistant materials instead of textiles and do not mess around. They are hard and sturdy, being made of wood or metal, and fit the window exactly. When closed, therefore, such shutters give the room a cast-iron opaqueness to the outside world and you cannot see your hand in front of your face. In the event of both clock hands pointing up to twelve, not that you would be able to see them, it would be impossible to gauge whether it were time you were in bed or time to be making some lunch.

In my experience – and I do not claim to possess an exhaustive knowledge of the field – shutters come in two main varieties. There are the wooden door-like ones that characterise the archetypal rustic dwelling in rural France. These can still let in the odd bit of light when closed, however unintentionally, perhaps through a crack in the wood. Alternatively, there are the high-tech electronically operated roller shutters, which create both pitch-darkness and a sense of being fastened inside a shipping container. Various handle-wound offerings sit somewhere between these extremes. This is not to mention the growingly prevalent 'plantation shutters' that increasingly grace the windows of the British upper-middle classes, advertising the household's socio-economic status in the absence of the family Range Rover when the latter has been deployed on the weekly Waitrose haul during the homeowners' periods of residency between medicinal skiing trips.

Shutters are often still accompanied by curtains. The functional and aesthetic balance of shutter to curtain depends on the type of shutter. The primitive wooden type might not actually be intended for use. Indeed, its moving parts might be severely decayed and there might be more transient decorations in its path obstructing movement in any case. If you try to close a shutter of this type, it might creak resistantly, fall off its hinges or indeed swipe a hanging basket off the outside wall, occasioning those below variously to experience startlement and life-threatening injury. If you experience this sort of outcome, you were almost certainly expected just to draw the curtains and leave the shutter alone. Roller shutters, on the other hand, are intended for nothing other than blocking out the light with industrial clarity. Where these are fitted, it is the curtains that are the cosmetic enhancement.

Ideally, since we don't all have shutters and might not think to look for them, your host will advise you of any that exist. I once stayed in a house where my host only happened to mention the shutters in conversation the night before I went home. I had been entirely unsuspicious of the presence of these things, which were activated by an almost invisible switch that was hidden by some decorative curtains. I had been forcing said curtains, which were of the skimpy and near-transparent type, into service. This meant that I had woken up every morning at about 4:30. On the final night, I marvelled as the room was consumed by total darkness as the shutters purred closed. The following morning, I dozily snoozed my alarm, slept for a further two hours and nearly missed my train home. This was partly owing to the exclusion of light and partly because I was still somewhat fatigued from three days of being awake at the crack of dawn, courtesy of the translucent curtains.

I once stayed on the ground floor of a quaint cottage that fronted straight onto a narrow pavement in a winding village. The windows were equipped with old-fashioned wooden shutters and no curtains. When throwing open the shutters in the morning, I unthinkingly did so into a procession of metal-stick-wielding ramblers who instinctively dived into the road to avoid my splintery assault. I apologised profusely but they were too busy doing the same to the Ocado van driver, who in turn had had to swerve to avoid flattening them. The walkers also struggled to hear my penitential pleas owing to their inability to take turns when clarifying to me what a careless imbecile I was. I was later struck by just how easy it would have been for some impish cockwomble, strolling past before I had opened up for the day, to have opened one of my shutters, knocked on the window and shouted 'boo!' or similar before running off to boast to their like-minded chums about their morning's intellectual accomplishment. Thanks to my spatial naïvety, I now had a list of suspects for if I were to fall victim to such a wheeze.

SIX

Housekeeping

If you are staying the night in someone else's home, however spontaneous, extraordinary or mundane the circumstances, it is almost certain that at some point you are going to take off your clothes. Indeed, it would be more idiosyncratic and, in a limited number of cases, a source of considerable disappointment, if you didn't. Once you've removed your clothes, if we are to assume that they haven't been tossed aside with lustful abandon, what exactly do you do with them?

I always used to work on the basis that the guest room would inevitably be embarrassingly unkempt as long as I was the incumbent and that that was okay so long as I guaranteed to leave it spotless upon my departure. As a slovenly yet well-intentioned adolescent with, now I look back, an untenable shortage of self-awareness, I never really thought it offensive to be leaving clothes around the place in a guest room. I was existing in a private environment designated to me. My disorderly habits wouldn't affect my host because they wouldn't be going in there during my stay anyway and I would leave the place as I had found it. However, the more people I was lucky enough to be able to stay with as the years unfolded, the more uncomfortably aware I became of my hosts trying but ultimately failing to suppress appalled gasps and facial expressions upon catching a glimpse through my open bedroom door and beholding the devastated and shit-strewn wasteland that I had created in their previously homely and inviting space. Unattractively, I tended to occupy a room for less than half an hour before it started to present as being lived in by a man unable to look after himself. The mild wincing on the part of some hosts suggested a fear that my whirlwind of garments and other detritus would still be there after I'd gone home. Perhaps it might even be necessary to redecorate after my departure, their startled expressions seemed to fear. The realisation that my innocent teenage sloppiness had the potential to be interpreted as thuggish contempt prompted me to evaluate my conduct, thankfully just before it occurred to anyone to demand a security deposit in advance of my visit.

In many bedrooms, there is a chair on which you can conveniently station your clothes without making a mess of either the room or the garments. Such a chair might well be furnished with cushions or be acting as a throne for a teddy bear or similar cuddly companion. It is up to one's sentimentality about such creatures as to whether one piles up one's clothes on top of the bear or feels sufficiently whimsical as to move him or her to prevent suffocation. If there is no chair and I don't wish to cram garments that are to be worn again back into my bag, potentially creasing them even more than they already emerged following my inept brand of ironing, it would of course seem unthinkably loutish and uncultivated for me to toss them down on the floor. However, if I do this after having first positioned a suitcase or holdall at the bottom of the pile of garments, I am now 'laying my clothes on my suitcase,' however swamped by clothes the suitcase might become and however much the apparel might, in practice, still be spilling onto the floor. This distinction enables me to appear house-trained and less caveman-like, at least to myself.

If you're staying somewhere for several nights, you may desire a more permanent holding for your garments, where they can breathe and you can wear them without projecting the impression of having slept in them along with five rescued cats. The clear solution here is to hang them in the wardrobe, inevitably then leaving them behind on departure. But what if there isn't a wardrobe? More ambiguously, what if there *is* one but it has not been explicitly sanctioned for your use? Is it taken for granted that you'll instinctively and unhesitatingly take advantage of it? I've always tended to assume not. Perhaps it depends on the storage capacity of the house in proportion to its number of occupants, and their characteristics. Many households use their spare bedrooms' wardrobes as overflow depositories for their own wares, especially when one half of a couple owns more than one shirt and so cannot possibly cram such an excessive hoard in amongst the voluminous fashion archive of their spouse. Consequently, the wardrobe in the guest room might not have the capacity to offer hospitality to the attire of fleeting visitors.

One wonders if it constitutes a gross violation of one's host's privacy to so much as *open* the wardrobe without their expressed consent. I once innocently let myself into the guest-room wardrobe when staying with a couple. I anticipated a glimpse of a few of the most mundane cubic metres of the house: an empty rail on which might have been hung a modest offering of the household's least treasured coat hangers, perhaps a formal overcoat worn on solemn occasions and maybe a shelf serving as the final resting place of something wholesome but obsolete, such as an atlas. Instead, however, I happened upon an absorbing (not that I hung around to soak it up fully) selection of regalia that I believe qualified as 'kinky'. There are some tendencies one doesn't attribute to certain people but my imagination was now dragging me, despite my protestations, into an ultra-high-definition scene in which I very much felt like the third wheel. I started to understand why one of my hosts had recently needed a heart operation. There was also a truncheon and a pair of handcuffs, which vaguely made sense as heirlooms because I believe the man's father had been in the police force.

Since making these improbable findings, I've tended to think of wardrobes as an exclusion zone around the perimeter of the room, prisons of secrets and arresting articles (especially in the case of the handcuffs) that one cannot unsee. On a similar motif, it is probably not the done thing to enter your host's drawers without an unambiguous invitation. Rare exceptions can be made if they are the drawers of someone with whom you are exceptionally closely acquainted or perhaps if you belong to the Gideons.

If you are sleeping in a communal area, your suitcase will be an island upon which will be stationed your entire life for the duration of your stay. It might be tucked away somewhere during the day where it won't look unsightly or surprise your host by coercing them into an involuntary somersault when they come down for breakfast. Your case might be stored behind the sofa or under a table, but your meticulously house-proud host could equally have whisked it away to an undisclosed upstairs location while you've gone for a shower and not yet unpacked the day's clean pants. There are parallels with the aforementioned suitcase-based clothes piles, or 'floordrobes' if we are to be down with the proverbial kids. When I am in the position of needing to keep all my possessions in, on or next to a bag or suitcase, I find that my things initially form a steeply ascending mountain which eventually suffers a landslide and consumes most of the available floor space. The room experiences an indoor version of high tide, where the glimmering salt water of the sea has been replaced with my trousers. People comment that their houses feel bigger after I've gone. Obviously, it goes down well if certain items are excluded from the pile in the interests of good taste. Householders may eventually pass comment, for instance, when their vista of *Eastenders* is defiled by an exhibition of yesterday's Y-fronts.

Another important bit of housekeeping is the business of keeping your bed (or equivalent) presentable during the day. If you're staying in a communal area, you might well need to clear your nest away in the morning and set it up again the following bedtime. If you're staying in a bedroom, there will by definition be a bed to make. For me, this used to be much the same as the scenario with my clothes: I cleaned up my act when I felt the disdain from hosts who got a snapshot of my dishevelled and chaotic duvet as they crossed the landing.

You might be sleeping on a bed that you found decorated with cushions and it may not seem necessary to replace the cushions each morning. That said, in practice, you will need to transfer them back from the floor to the bed in order to be able to carve out a path to the door, for which you will need to set your alarm to go off approximately twenty minutes earlier than it would otherwise.

One rather rare but crucial set of circumstances in which you should go the extra mile to keep your room tidy is, as I once discovered, when your host's house happens to be up for sale. I stayed for a couple of months in a house that was on the market and managed to hinder the sale in more ways than I would have thought my meek and retiring presence could have made possible.

My being a longer-term guest, my room was in a rather more lived-in state than most people – even I – can usually achieve when merely staying one or two nights. I had rather more than one room's worth of items in the modest space. I was occupying a distant attic bedroom and my elderly host could rarely summon the energy or the inclination to ascend the flights of stairs to check that I hadn't started growing cannabis or smuggled in a pet hen. However, she made an exception when showing the estate agent's photographer to my bedroom one morning without prior warning. There came a knock on the door, which I unguardedly answered without the circumspection of one who is simultaneously about to be papped by a suited gentleman with a Nikon wide-angle lens and reprimanded by his landlady for having eclipsed the carpet with his personal effects.

It was agreed, using words that were few in number but robust in impact, that the vibe I had going in the room was not going to enhance the value of the property. I contritely and hurriedly bulldozed everything out of sight, so that the room could be captured on film before being doubled in size via the appropriate software in preparation for the advert's release. I would, of course, have done this before the paparazzi had arrived at my door and made me feel so fleetingly important, had I received the aforementioned prior warning.

Despite my poor housekeeping having threatened to defile the photographs, the advert for the house subsequently appeared in the public domain. The next episode on these premises therefore saw a prospective buyer coming to look around. Happily, this occurred after a couple of weeks or so. The proprietor decided it wise to alert me to the impending visit this time, sensing that it would make for a more comfortable and profitable experience for all concerned and improve the chances of her not having to live there for the rest of her life. The night before the viewing, therefore, my host kindly informed me that the estate agent would be bringing the interested party around the following afternoon. Conscious that my room was edging its way back to the free-and-easy condition it had been in when threatened by the photographer's lens, I assured my host that I'd make things tidy for the punters.

'Oh no, you don't need to worry about that,' she smiled sweetly. 'They'll only look around your bedroom door quickly and they're here to see the house, not your things!'

I wasn't fooled by her external breeziness and thought it best to do a bit of a clear-up. I knew what the consequences of not doing so could be following a scenario a few years earlier, where I had accompanied a friend to a viewing of a flat. The outgoing tenants of said flat were a good deal more disorderly in their homemaking than even I was in this room now. Underpants flowed abundantly from drawers and collected in piles on the floor beneath, while a rabble of used crockery densely occupied the kitchen worktop and cried out for an army of scouring pads and a petrol tanker of Fairy liquid. The flat was spacious, well-located and available for a very reasonable monthly sum. Despite this, my friend declined it because she couldn't get past the underpants and dirty plates, somehow unable to believe that they'd be gone before the start of her tenancy. Tidying my room now, therefore, did not strike me as optional. I had no wish for my slovenliness to wreak such profound havoc on my host's odds of selling her home and vowed to spend the morning making the place a haven of uncluttered order. The house would be sold at first glance and the new owners would perhaps want to pay me to live there and maintain the other rooms to a standard as high as that which I had attained in my own.

Regrettably, it was not to be. I exited the bathroom after my morning shower, wearing an abysmally skimpy towel, to the jarring sight of an arc of humans gathered around my bedroom door. A sharply dressed family of five was being given the forecasted *afternoon* tour of the premises a little after 9 AM. The adults peered into my room but did not dare to step inside, as if it were a carefully curated museum display that showcased an alternative way of living. Two things were immediately apparent about my host, the first being that she thought 'morning' was merely a synonym for 'afternoon,' and the second being that she had been polite to the point of self-defeat when telling me that she didn't need me to tidy up. The estate agent and viewers, who had already been looking at the room with politely disguised horror as if suspecting its occupant to have been featured in a Channel 4 documentary, terminated their visual assault course and probably my host's prospect of a sale by turning their heads towards the documentary's damp and enfeebled protagonist, who was now struggling to mask his assets with his towel. The designer-tweed-clad mother inadequately tried to shield her children from me while the agent attempted a touchingly irrelevant exultation of the property's original oak panelling. Drawing parallels with my friend on her apartment viewing, there now appeared a sudden keenness on the viewers' part for confirmation not only that my detritus would be gone in the event of a purchase, but that I would be too.

SEVEN

Beds

The centrepiece of any bedroom tends to be the bed. This is therefore the principal object of investigation when meeting a bedroom for the first time. Your first sight of the bed, or indeed whatever equivalent furnishing has been offered for your repose, is the first impression of your level of comfort for the night ahead. It gives you an idea of the amount of sleep you are likely to get and enables you to hazard an educated guess as to whether or not you will be able to straighten your neck or stand in an approximately symmetrical fashion the next day.

The luckiest guest will arrive at a luxurious double bed with a supple yet cosseting mattress. The only real decision to be made here is the side on which to sleep. It has already been suggested that this matter might be decided according to which side features a vacant plug socket, but there are other factors too. If you choose to sleep in the middle, you can starfish in an indulgent manner but being such a vast distance from any of the bed's edges could result in the sensation of being washed up and stranded on a vast cotton beach. Alternatively, the force of habit might incline you towards the side you'd sleep on at home or, unhindered by the prescriptive presence of your partner, you might choose to bask in the novelty of sprawling out across the marital fault-line.

If you are sleeping in a big and comfy double bed in a room prepared by a host with an especially pious devotion to soft furnishings, you may well need to engage in a ritual of superfluous-cushion removal before you can consider getting into bed. The practice of the bed being decorated with a varied assortment of cushions during daylight hours is a source of twilight angst for many a partner. No one is spending time in the bedroom while these things are out on display, or if they are it isn't to admire the textiles. These cushions are like the ornamental curtains one often finds; someone invented something useful and then many centuries later it got hijacked as an aesthetic folly that was then rarely used for its intended purpose.

Rather like the cooking of Christmas dinner, the cushion regime turns getting into bed into an activity which requires some significant manual labour before one can reap the delights of the finished product. Attempts to achieve entry to the bed resemble an archaeological dig, as the cushions that have crowned the empty and ignored bedroom all day have to be cleared away before the bedroom can fulfil its rôle.

The cushions tend to be arranged as if trying to impersonate a formation of the Red Arrows. They spend the day in neat and patient rows like members of an audience at the theatre or passengers standing attentively on a platform awaiting a train. It would be easy to imagine them with faces, either showing solemn appreciation for the performance they were watching or complaining about the waiting time. Once night falls, it is your job to serve them with their twice-daily dose of attention.

Starting with the front row, perhaps a metre and a half south of the headboard, you might first remove a central cushion of severe landscape orientation, a similar size to a Monopoly box and usually of some firmness. Behind that will be two square cushions with dimensions comparable to large briefcases, of a different texture and level of resistance – excessively fluff-laden, perhaps, or with a shiny appearance – in a colour that wittily complements the item that was in front. Behind these will perhaps be another three cushions, different again but no less essential to the artistic makeup of the bed. These might be wildly patterned, or feature buttons to repel anyone who might wish to use them for purposes of resting their head. By this point, the setup evokes the formation that the Red Arrows refer to as the Big Nine. However, the Red Arrows can only dream of constellations on the scale of the cushion fiesta because they are sadly limited to nine aeroplanes.

Move back another row and you find yourself graduating from cushions to pillows, although it will still be a while before striking anything on which your skull can spend the night. In my experience, this stage is often where tassels come in, in a ticklish blaze of lengths and colours, although I believe the rubric also permits their introduction further to the front. This is especially the case when making a bed in one of the Home Counties or during the week of the Epiphany. Eventually, you get to the pillows that are designed to accommodate the human head overnight, but you have to remove at least two of these as well so that your head won't be forced to spend the night at ninety degrees from the rest of you. You may even have had to remove some sort of teddy bear from a perch atop this upholstered oasis, the stuffed creature having spent the last fifteen minutes either showing you sympathy or silently critiquing your every move.

Once you've unearthed the functional pillow, you look around and realise that the room has now effectively been transformed into a soft play area, there now being somewhere between twelve and eighty-seven cushions and pillows on the floor. In a small room containing a double bed, this means the loss of an overwhelming percentage of the total floor space.

What should you do with all these cushions now? If you leave them where they've landed, you will almost certainly trip over at least seven of them if you get up in the night, consequently headbutting the wardrobe and knocking yourself out. That said, they could be useful for padding the floor in case you fall out of bed or, should something more hair-raising occur during the night, they could be thrown out of the window to soften your landing on the driveway below. It is likely, however, that you will simply want them out of the way.

The night-time storage of redundant cushions is a source of such universal anxiety that people have written articles advising solutions for those whose lives are blighted by such conundrums, seemingly unsuspicious that the blame for such an overbearing textile situation may lie uncomfortably close to home. The author of one such article – and some people will probably consider this to be only sensible – suggests purchasing a chest to be kept at the foot of the bed for no purpose other than to be filled with cushions while you are unconscious. By day, such a chest would be entirely empty. I can think of a thrifty way of short-circuiting the whole business.

Anyway, whatever you decide to do with the things overnight, the next morning you will need to reassemble the entire *objet d'art* upon the bed, starting at the headboard and working south. You would be wise to take a photo of the layout the night before to ensure an accurate reproduction.

Another possible use of the additional pillows and cushions is the padding out of your environment against potential hazards. Spare rooms are often retirement homes for furniture that is surplus to requirements. Your bedside table, therefore, could be an oversized item with sharp corners. Said corners could protrude into your personal space and touch your pillow, creating a painfully resistant endangerment against which you could strike yourself in the night. Not so, however, if you have a velvet paisley number lodged between the bed and the potential point of concussion. Similarly, it happens all too often that the pillow you're actually using disappears down the back of the bed. The risk of this can be eliminated if you have stuffed the gap behind your head with a puffy yarn cotton item with tricolour pom-poms.

You might be sleeping in a bed that has sheets instead of or as well as a duvet. Where this is the case, many hosts like to make the room so neat and photogenic that the sheet is inexplicably tightly tucked in, as one might find in a hotel. This is often executed to a point where inserting oneself beneath the sheet resembles opening a tin of paint with a knife. It can be difficult to break in at all. It could possibly be useful to pack a spade or other proportionally sized implement to prize open the linen, operated of course with the lightest possible touch. Admittedly, you would need to be prepared to answer questions as you made your way upstairs with such an unlikely and mildly sinister instrument sticking out of the top of your overnight bag. Once you have managed to post yourself into bed when the sheets are installed in this way, you are rigidly strapped to the mattress, as if simultaneously wearing three seat belts and a straitjacket.

You will need to fine-tune your sense of spatial awareness if you are accustomed to sleeping on a double bed at home and now find yourself horizontal for the night on a single. Turning over in a single bed needs to be done with greater precision. In order to remain safely aboard, you might need to rotate on an axis that runs down the centre of your body. This contrasts with the less exacting arrangement in a double bed where you can liberally hurl your body from one side to the other as if creating a mirror image on the other side of a line of symmetry. Attempting such freedom of movement in a single bed will likely result in your crossing ending at a severely lower altitude than where it started, almost certainly with a bit of a bump. It is to be hoped that you can remain aware of this danger while you're asleep, lest you wake up dazed and bruised on the floor. It is rather like when a bus driver wedges a double-decker bus under a low bridge before claiming that they thought they were in a single-decker. At least making a spatial misjudgment in the bedroom isn't going to end up being passed around the internet courtesy of the footage from someone's dashcam or equivalent. Indeed, if there is any possibility of this happening, you have far bigger things to worry about than falling out of bed.

If you're spending the night in a space that is normally used for something other than sleeping, you might find yourself parked on a folding bed. These are not designed for the good of one's long-term spinal wellbeing – although I did sleep on one every night for three months and can still stand up approximately normally –

but they can certainly sustain a weary traveller through a few nights in reasonable if confined comfort. Their dimensions, proximity to the floor and slightly flimsy nature mean that one must board in a slightly more controlled and delicate fashion than one might with a more permanent bed. It is sensible to be conservative when committing one's entire body weight to the structure because sometimes, people – notably those who will not be sleeping on such a thing themselves – are not awfully particular about whether the legs have been properly unfolded. If care has not been taken during assembly, the whole construction will cheekily collapse beneath you with invigorating speed and clamour. Unless you are in residence on the Moon, it is highly likely that you will go down with it. In an ideal world, the ten-centimetres-thick mattress would cushion your back and legs from the worst of the metal poles and struts onto which you have crash-landed. In reality, you might end up needing to be carried out disfigured on a stretcher, when someone eventually finds you, and having to take a fortnight off work. Of course, the most prudent approach is simply to check that the legs are correctly configured *before* getting in. The decision to bother doing this might be based on whether or not you're entitled to sick pay. This is also something you will need to consider if you are in the habit of turning over in bed. It is ironic that a folding bed is not usually decked out with the array of cushions and similar protective resources that often grace a plump and cosseting double bed because these are the circumstances where you're most likely to need something to break your fall.

Even if your body is safely supported from underneath, there might be something resistant lurking above your head. Maybe you are sleeping in a loft room where the bed has been slotted under the sloping roof in a manner that would be considered unsustainably concussive for permanent occupants but deemed acceptable for a robustly skulled person staying for one night. The bed might alternatively have been placed in close proximity to a charming but inflexible exposed beam.

The most hazardous bed type of all is, of course, the bunk bed. Both the altitude of the top bunk and the flimsiness of the ladder offer the same levels of danger to the inexperienced as tightrope-walking and flame-throwing, but the peril doesn't stop there. Unthinkingly sitting up on the bottom bunk will result in a severe head injury, while sitting up on the higher bunk may do likewise if the ceiling is at a low altitude. This is to say nothing of what nocturnal unrest might occur if the other bunk is simultaneously occupied. The glass of water on the bedside table comes to the rescue in these situations to facilitate the taking of any painkillers you may thoughtfully have packed. In the process of accessing it and them, you might do yourself such a devastating mischief on your descent from the top bunk that you end up skipping the drugs and simply telephoning for an ambulance instead.

EIGHT

Sleeping in a Communal Area

It could well be that you are a welcome (or otherwise) addition to an already-full house, in which case you might be sleeping somewhere that is not ordinarily intended for overnight repose. Where this is the case, you will be somewhat more vulnerable. You will have less control over your space and be exposed to a plethora of inane scenarios that wouldn't darken the doorstep of a sealed spare bedroom. For instance, you might be holed up in the living room, in which case bedtime will only happen when everyone else has vacated the area for the night. I remember once being involved in a game of Monopoly that was taking place in the room in which I would eventually have been sleeping. Having started the game clean-shaven, many hours later I was stroking my long beard and desperately trying to lose in order that time might have been called on the whole thing. It had now exceeded four in the morning and nobody had been that arsed about playing in the first place.

Since being stationed for the night in a communal area often means that everyone else drifts away and you stay put, there's a feeling of the space being signed over to you for the night. It's prudent to remember that your privacy, while respected by other householders, will not be absolute. Reception rooms often have panes of glass in the doors. It is therefore wise to be self-aware when removing your pants and so on, lest unprepared passers-by in the hallway end up concluding their evening on the receiving end of a full moon. Such a cheeky display could be interpreted as a petty gesture of poor sportsmanship on the back of your having just lost a game of Monopoly. That said, should your audience be the person who dragged their fictional property-trading tycoonery out until sunrise to ensure a victory over their less fanatical opponents, a quick gluteal gesticulation to see them on their way is probably justified.

Further to these words of caution, it is perhaps advisable to leave a window of at least ten minutes before you start to undress, in order that people have the opportunity to return to the room to retrieve items that they may have left behind. For instance, you may feel the niggling possibility as you strip off that someone might rejoin you in pursuit of the mobile phone that you now suddenly notice awaiting its owner on the chair arm. Having said that, people returning to the room for whatever reason do not necessarily do so in the same state of dignified apparel as that in which they left, even when it's only been a few minutes.

I was once hosted in a small French apartment by a charming twenty-something lady who, the second night I was there, had her boyfriend staying. We all spent a thoroughly convivial time as they introduced me to the local sausage – a regional andouillette recipe with ingredients that they advised me not to Google – and we took turns subjecting each other to our favourite music before retiring to bed. I was sleeping in the living room and the remnants of the soirée's various bottled beverages remained on the coffee table while I spent ten minutes idly scrolling through social media after the couple had departed (with enthusiastic urgency) for the bedroom. I looked up from my phone not many minutes later to the unforeseen sight of the well-sculpted gentleman standing a metre in front of me, wearing nothing but a skimpy and conceitedly snug pair of underpants. Indeed, his minimalistic attire combined with Our Lord having looked after him in the photogenic-body stakes suggested that he had walked in fresh from the pages of *Pants and Muscles Monthly*. He appeared still to be enjoying his evening, as inescapably demonstrated by the strained garment's struggle to contain his excitement. Fearing the worst for the resilience of the material, and indeed, therefore, fearing the *wurst,* my panicked eyes sought to save themselves by focussing hard on a nearby vase of daffodils in order to avoid meeting the second local sausage of the evening. Meanwhile, the Gallic fellow gestured to the two large bottles of mineral water on the table.

'Steel or sparkleeng?'

'Um, still,' I replied, slightly stupefied. He then withdrew, taking the bottle of still water with him and leaving me with the sparkling. This wasn't the outcome I'd anticipated, even with the tiny portion of my brain cells that could manage an opinion on the mineral water after computing everything else. It is unlikely, I hope, that I would have met the man in such an immodest state if I had been secluded in a spare bedroom.

This sense of being unshielded from the activities of other people in communal spaces continues into the morning. Depending on the intimacy of your acquaintance with your host, being awake before they enter the room isn't essential so long as you're not overly sensitive about what you wake up to or how. I once spent the night on a sofa in an apartment shared with some friends who had excitedly agreed at bedtime that the next day would begin with a pre-breakfast yoga session. This would take place in the living room where I, the person invigorated neither by mornings nor voluntarily induced pain, would be sleeping. I woke up fenced in by a row of studiously balanced and skyward-facing posteriors. It was a profoundly unorthodox situation and I didn't quite know what to do with myself. It was fragrantly apparent that the application of deodorant was a rite that had been put on hold until after breakfast. Beyond my control, my sleeping space had been transformed into a moral high ground of torture as my legging-clad cohabitants let out ideologically satisfied sounds of muscular torment. I almost joined in with their songs of discomfort because I needed to relieve myself but couldn't get past the holistic spectacle without disturbing the choreography. I had previously been told with some sternness that I wasn't allowed to make a commentary on the situation, which was a bit of a tall order.

Sleeping in a communal area can make you feel self-conscious about obstructing key facilities of the home, or at least uneasily aware that you might wake up as a docile traffic island surrounded by people making coffee. The rich bass notes of your snoring might serenade the entire family at the breakfast table. I have frequently slept on sofas in apartments where the living room and kitchen are combined, inducing an uneasy awareness that I am hampering free-and-easy access to the kitchen facilities. This is an especially pressing matter if staying in a household where someone is going to work early the next morning and needs to be in the kitchen at a time you'd rather not be awake. If this is someone you don't know very well or a member of the household other than the person who has invited you, they might be worried about disturbing you and you might be discomfited about the prospect of an audience as you lie unconscious on their furniture, possibly snoring or drooling in an unalluring manner. The only remedy for this early morning incompatibility is to set an alarm for 5:30 AM and doze for three hours with one eye open before your host eventually appears and reveals that they have the day off.

It could be that you are not remotely obstructing the household facilities because you do not have access to them yourself, which is a source of even greater consternation than a mild loss of privacy. I once stayed with a friend in a flat that was split between two floors of a big Victorian house. The downstairs front room contained the kitchen and living room while the bedroom and en-suite bathroom were located on the first floor and accessed via the building's communal staircase. I was sleeping downstairs. The fact that the bathroom was only accessible via the hosts' bedroom meant that I had to relieve myself once and for all before bed because the utility would then be out of bounds until morning. I couldn't respectably let myself into the bedroom of my friend and his other half just to have a pee, which was especially unfortunate when the evening had witnessed the intake of a destabilizing quantity of beer in celebration of the feast of my friend's nativity. In any case, the bedroom door was secured with a Yale lock. Maybe they'd had problems before. I felt like I was making an impossible commitment on behalf of my bladder as we all bade each other goodnight and the bedroom door clicked shut.

Increasingly consumed with impending doom, I lay awake with the niggling worry that the next wave of poncy artisan ale would soon start to lap against the floodgates, and almost instantly it did. Or did it? If I'd had unlimited access to the WC, the feeling probably wouldn't have struck so soon, suggesting that this present sensation could merely have been born out of anxiety. Furthermore, my friends and I were in a trade-off of amenities. Just as I was being prevented from accessing the bathroom, so had my presence downstairs largely cordoned the kitchen off from my hosts. I could have baked a cake, washed my clothes or made and drunk any number of cups of tea that would have rendered my discomfort even more acute. However, none of this unbounded domestic possibility quite compensated for the agony of having to, as per the metaphorical prose of James Bay, 'hold back the river'. The best solution would have been a half-time meeting at 3 AM, where they could have come downstairs for a slice of the cake I'd made while they slept and I could have nipped upstairs to eliminate urine. Naturally, this flash of ingenuity only struck me after we'd gone to bed when I couldn't suggest the idea for the same reason that I couldn't let myself into the bathroom. I'm surprised I didn't wet myself with the sheer complexity of it all. Turns out 'help yourself to anything from the bathroom,' i.e. a piss, would be a much more practical nicety than the relatively gimmicky freedom to pour yourself a glass of elderflower cordial at half three in the morning.

Although it is usually the guest who ends up sleeping in a communal area, I once experienced the reverse situation in which a host in France apparently didn't trust this wild Englishman unsupervised in a room with knives and butter and so slept on a sofa bed in the apartment's kitchen-diner and gave me the adjoining room. She sealed herself inside the communal living space and went to sleep before I realised that I'd left my phone on the kitchen worktop. I ended up resigned to being apart from my phone for the night, which I dare say would have done me good had it not been for the resulting lack of an alarm clock. I left the curtains open and relied on being awoken by the sunlight, meaning of course that I didn't go to sleep properly at all just in case I ended up missing the next day. My host, a Hungarian tennis coach no less, was devoted to an efficient and exuberant morning routine that somehow both maximised sleep and allowed time for things like a dawn jog, or whatever it is that sporty people do before devotedly unhurried people like me are usually conscious. I was aiming to get ready for the day while she was out running, in order to be presentable to her on her return. Regrettably, a prospective piano pupil decided that this was the morning on which they would telephone me before sunrise to enquire about lessons, thus taking the first brave step on their musical journey. Consequently, I was woken not by rays of light streaming into the room but by my host being tasered from slumber by my ringtone and unleashing an immediate torrent of such heartfelt phrases as 'fuck you' in Hungarian ('bazdmeg,' should you wish to experiment at home). My nervously pointing out that she now had time for an even longer run in the morning's favourable conditions almost saw me extinguished.

Tangentially, as a result of a better-natured conversation about linguistic quirks that we shared later in the day, I can report that it is commonplace for a testy Hungarian to hurl a weighty 'Szarjál sünt!' into the face of an opponent, meaning 'May you shit a hedgehog'. It would follow that there might be an ancient Hungarian proverb along the lines of 'pricks get pricks' but I have no evidence that there is.

Some people are so flamboyantly lacking in precaution that they appear impervious to received wisdom. I would have thought one of the most basic rudiments of sleeping in a communal part of someone else's home would be that it is sensible to wear something to avoid advertising your more private anatomical commodities, even if you're not carrying your usual sleepwear. However, one hears frightful stories from those whose guests have regarded being covered by the duvet as an alternative to wearing clothes. Such guests are gravely mistaken. If you are sleeping on someone's sofa, you have to honour their kind hospitality by not defiling the furniture with your bare arse. Moreover, they *will* find out. When they enter the living room at 9 AM to find that your duvet has fallen to the floor while you are spread out comatose in your birthday suit, there is no defence.

Another ingredient of the communal-area sleeping experience might be that you are spending the night on something more improvised or temporary than a conventional bed...

NINE

Airbeds

If you are staying in a house that lacks a spare bedroom but where someone has graciously and sacrificially offered to put you up in any case, your host will be faced with the challenge of finding you a makeshift sleeping solution. One possibility might be an airbed.

Unless I misjudge my readership, it is unlikely that you are intimately versed in the history of airbeds. It is also unlikely that you give a mole-rat's derrière about it, but since you're here I'll treat you. Contrary to a view you may have held that the airbed was an innovation of recent decades, recorded appearances of them exist from as early as the nineteenth century. A learned gentleman named Ernie Smith, with whose research I couldn't possibly compete, tells us via a website called *Atlas Obscura* that one of the earliest references to such an item is from 1850. One Margaret Frink, making the journey from Indiana to California that year during the gold rush, recounts sleeping on an Indian-rubber mattress that could be filled with air or water. She reports that it was a 'very comfortable bed'. That said, she and her husband, Ledyard, were travelling the best part of two thousand miles and so probably weren't all that arsed about the more trifling nuances of lumbar support. At one point they spent thirty-seven hours in the 'frightful' desert and so the standards they expected possibly dipped below those of the average Hilton hotel patron.

Various enterprising people in the nineteenth century conceived of developments of the air mattress with varying degrees of ingenuity and commercial success. Ernie Smith continues that the earliest patent he can find of an air mattress is from 1853, registered by a man called John Scott, who married the comfort of fabric to the firmness and durability of an inflatable. Towards the end of the nineteenth century, a number of outfits began to market the concept, extolling the benefits of a firmness-adjustable mattress for those suffering from back pain. Although very similar to the airbeds of today, these were sold as mattresses to be used atop standard bed frames and slept on every night. Things sort of went from there. It's the type of subject on which would be written a volume for the endearingly niche collections of books one finds in garden centres and stately home gift shops, like French tea cosies of the 1900s or the development of the lamppost between the two world wars.

Anyway, enough academia. What comes down must first have gone up, and so if you're sleeping on an airbed there's the rite of inflation to complete before you can so much as think about settling down for the night. This is assuming the bed hasn't been blown up before your arrival but, since airbeds are usually laid on in communal areas owing to there being no devoted sleeping room available, the setting up of the bed will often not happen until the living room or wherever is vacated. If it's a more primitive airbed that needs to be pumped manually, the inflation session consists of an awkward sharing of teamwork because both host and guest feel a need to contribute despite it being firmly a one-person job. The host typically takes the lead – it is their airbed after all – and, emitting murmurings ranging from the mildly inquisitive to the wholly confounded, connects the inflation device in a temperamental manner. They then start to pump away furiously and noisily while you stand there attempting to dilute your guilt by wearing a look of deep concentration to show high engagement with the situation. At intervals, you emphasize that you are more than happy to pump yourself (indeed, you might well find it satisfying) while they become increasingly red in the face and start to perspire immoderately. The bed, meanwhile, lies soggily on the floor, hopelessly unfirm and discrediting the physical effort that is being poured into it. It is like trying to fell an oak tree with a cheese knife. You are ill at ease as your host insists there's no need to help, even though they're about to have an asthma attack. This prompts an attempt on your part to relieve the uneasy dynamic with a gesture of contrived assistance, such as unfolding the pillow cases or trying to fluff out the reluctant mattress. This scenario can play out for anything up to forty-five minutes, depending on the pumper's stamina and whether or not they have any underlying medical conditions. Your host may alternate between decreasingly restrained outbursts of intemperate language, insistences that they're 'fine' and the odd spot of passing out.

If your host is in a more regular habit of entertaining overnight guests on premises with no spare bedroom, they might well own a fancy-pants airbed complete with a built-in electronic pump. Indeed, they might simply own a separate electronic pump for entirely parallel reasons. Either way, it is significantly less physically involving when electricity is used and it also carries the neat advantage of the bed inflating in a manner so timely that you actually have a chance to sleep on it before sunrise. Vacuuming at midnight is considered antisocial but turning on an equally raucous pump to inflate an airbed is, apparently, perfectly fine. The airbed will often be placed in the middle of the living room, in the zone that would usually be the crossing between the room's points of interest: television, sofa, fireplace and so on. It is important to ensure that the space is clear before you start, as I learned a couple of years ago when being hosted in a grand Victorian living room in Edinburgh. My friend appeared at the appropriate time with an opulent double airbed. A fairly high-end item, it self-inflated with tremendous efficiency when plugged into the mains. We stood and watched in satisfied wonder for about twenty seconds until the thing started to swell almost beyond the capacity of the room, like a loaf of bread to which had been added too much yeast. We hastily extinguished the lit candles on the hearth as the bed engulfed more and more of the herringbone floor, eventually trapping us up against the wall by our shins.

Perhaps the most obvious downside to airbeds is their tendency to deflate overnight, causing you to wake up at 4 AM with various lumber complaints while shipwrecked in a non-cushioning pool of flaccid rubber. You will experience rock-hard discomfort even more quickly if you do not lie precisely in the middle of the bed. It is frequently impractical to start performing a nocturnal re-inflation operation for reasons of noise pollution, as well as the fact that several hours of lying in this position have rendered you unable to stand. An awareness of the location of the sodding pump might also be lacking.

Thus, if you find yourself lying on the floor surrounded by the deflated remains of your mattress yet still with five hours to kill until it's time to get up, all you can do is use the time to start writing your first novel or sneak out of the house and check into a hotel, returning in time for breakfast of course.

Pumps aside, it is quite astounding how much noise the airbed itself can generate. In the aforementioned Hungarian tennis coach's apartment, I spent my sleepless night in exile from the kitchen on an airbed that I think might actually have been a flotation device purchased in a holiday resort. I lowered myself onto the bed and it responded with the most outrageous cacophony imaginable. Each time I moved, the apartment reverberated to the sound of a tidal wave of polyvinyl chloride. It was surely enough to have awoken anyone above or below, next door or in Luxembourg. Feeling I needed to minimize this pandemonium was the second reason, along with the fatal mislaying of my alarm, for my spending the night frozen in a state of wide-eyed stillness. It is surprising with hindsight that my host didn't wake up much earlier and loudly implore me to shit a hedgehog but I suppose such a spiky excretion would have done irreparable harm to her noisy inflatable.

It is very good indeed if the other occupants of the house remember, or indeed are made aware in the first place, that they have a temporary resident spending the night at low altitude in a reception room. A friend once recounted an incident that occurred when his host's good lady arrived home from a late shift as a nurse, having not been kept abreast of the evening's arrangements. Their first acquaintance was when she entered the dark living room, tripped over the airbed therein and unceremoniously collapsed into bed with my startled friend, surprising him to consciousness with her intimate crash landing. The nurse's beloved, who coincided with all this after having come downstairs to greet her, felt understandably moved to pose direct questions to her and my friend about why they were horizontal in such proximity after dark. 'I fell' was of course the truthful explanation but somehow these words always bear a degree of inadequacy. The same excuse was once used by a vicar who arrived at Accident and Emergency with a potato lodged up his fundament. It is perhaps sensible to fix a note to the door to warn of your presence if there's a chance of your stay being punctuated by the delivery of a black eye.

TEN

Sleeping on the Sofa

The experience of sleeping on the sofa can vary considerably from household to household. It is a fate typically associated with those who find themselves holding a different opinion from their partners and then naïvely and masochistically telling them so. A subsequent barring from the marital bed and a night on the sofa serve as a penitential sentence for the spouse who was officially wrong and bad, allowing them to spend the hours of darkness thinking about what they've done. Depending on the characteristics of the sofa, they might indeed spend the entire night contemplating their actions because the chances of actually sleeping are minimal, particularly if the disagreement was so severe that the evicted party has not been allowed to take any pillows or blankets with them. All this will ideally lead to the rehabilitation of the offender, who will contritely apologise the next morning and swear a personal oath never to express a point of view ever again.

Alternatively, if the sofa is an extravagant and plush item, what was supposed to be a punishment could end up as a reward. If this happens, instead of changing their behaviour, the scorned and relegated partner will continue to use and develop their assertive powers when disagreement occurs. This will, in time, cultivate a feisty and fearless character who knows that the worst outcome of holding their own in a disputation is a night in luxurious accommodation. The chastised will enjoy a luxurious proximity to the fridge and none of the snoring or duvet-hogging with which they contend when they've played things by the book. When the sinner's powers of persuasion have become excessively evolved, their penalty of solitude is likely to be extended further to the self-contained tranquillity of the car or the garden shed.

Sleeping on the sofa is also something that you may do as a guest, either in a small home or one holding lots of people. As with sleeping in any communal area, the living room becomes your temporary personal space for the night and reverts to belonging to everybody the next morning, as does the sofa on which you have been sleeping. If you have been spending the evening in the living room with your host, you might need to take a moment at bedtime to adjust to the sensation that the room is a place of solitude. You may experience a certain cognitive dissonance when removing your trousers in the same location where, only moments earlier, you and your hosts were watching *Gogglebox* together. The coffee table, on which the evening's drinks and snacks were placed, becomes your bedside table. You place your watch and jewellery down between the coasters that, only moments ago, hosted the beverages of the entire household. If you are struggling to make yourself at home and your luggage capacity has permitted such things, you might wish to place a framed family portrait atop the television or perhaps position your favourite cactus in your line of vision to make it feel more like your space. These visual tokens of solace might be the greatest concessions to comfort that you experience before sunrise.

Once you have prepared the room, your attention turns to the making of your nest. The quality of sleep you will enjoy during a night on a sofa, not to mention the state of your posture for the following three weeks, depends on the sofa's characteristics. The greatest deciding factor is whether it is a three-seater or a two. In either case, it is an advantage to be short, but a three-seater will usually ensure that people of least average height have sufficient length – always an advantage in bed. Ideally, the sofa will have arms that are flat and soft, meaning that you can rest your head as if on a pillow at one end while keeping your feet on approximately the same line of altitude at the other.

If you are working with a two-seater with solid, built-up arms and you are more than four foot six, you may have more of a problem. One option in this case is to curl up into the foetal position although the tall-of-stature will, in practice, find themselves folded up like the innards of a tuba. Alternatively, you can sleep with your head and torso in the trench between the sofa arms while your legs project diagonally into the air, supported by the sofa arm, so that they resemble planks of wood sticking out of a short pickup truck. Your feet may be exposed, vulnerable both to the cold and to opportunistic ticklers. On a table below your overhanging feet, there might be a vase which, in due course, you will successfully kick to the hardwood floor. It will probably contain the fresh flowers laid on for your visit along with two litres of water, which will soon be unrestrainedly dispersed across the room. The vase is probably a family heirloom or an expensive antique but in practice it doesn't matter whether it is of any value or not – you will shit yourself senseless on the off-chance after breaking it, even if it subsequently turns out to have been from the home department of Primark. Fortunately, you will be near the kitchen, where you will find absorbent cloths and perhaps a drawer containing superglue so that you can pass a tensely engrossing night of amateur ceramic restoration.

Anyway, I am getting ahead of myself. There is a great deal of preparation to do before you need to start contemplating the night-time position of your legs. The first job is to remove the cushions. The decorative after-market cushions (only now have I learned that they're called 'scatter cushions') on the sofa are at least likely to be fewer in number than those being wearily removed each night from the king-size beds of picture-perfect social media accounts, so you might still make it into bed before the cushion aficionado sleeping upstairs. Removing the cushions that form part of the sofa will provide a bit more depth and surface area to the sleeping platform. It may also unveil £7.23 in loose change and a remote control that has long outlived the device it once operated. I can tell from here that you are honest and reputable enough to return any found currency to your host the next morning without my patronisingly advising it but I nonetheless underline the importance of doing so in case the money has been deliberately planted to test your good character. One would hope it unlikely that a friend or relative would feel the need to conduct such an experiment but perhaps an Airbnb host might see it as a shrewd policy in order to determine whether guests might be allowed back. When I was a child, my mother had a cleaning company carry out a trial clean of our house and, halfway through the operation, one of the cleaners sought her out to report and hand over £5.20 that they'd ostensibly found while cleaning under the sofa cushions. I called bullshit on the whole thing as there was no way that £5.20 could have found its way overnight down the orifices of a sofa that, at the time, I checked daily for such tender. It was quite clearly the company's way of writing itself a glowing character reference while being wise to the idea that potential clients might put the organisation's integrity on trial in this manner. Regrettably, the company folded a short time later. This was presumably because it was giving all the profits away to potential clients via this eccentric charade. If this was indeed the case, it is no small irony that they put themselves out of business by proving their honesty via a routine that involved lying about having found things that were never there.

Once the cushions are dealt with and piled up on the floor, the lounge now resembling the bedroom of a cushion enthusiast who doesn't own a wooden chest, there's the matter of bedclothes. Many sofas are upholstered in leather, a material that is a status symbol in the context of a vehicular interior but which is not renowned for providing a hospitable sleeping surface. The provision of a sheet, an excellent item to flag up in the pre-lights-out 'do you have everything you need?' exchange, will reduce the chances of flatulent leathery sound effects and your waking up in a torrent of curiously adhesive sweat that results in your prizing yourself from the leather as if bound to it by body-length strips of Velcro. You will typically be covered by a duvet, which will decline to the floor as soon as you have fallen asleep. You might equally be contained by a sleeping bag, which will insulate you to great satisfaction throughout the night until you get up in a bleary-eyed state and forget that your legs are enveloped, causing you to stumble over the coffee table and start the day with a dazed close-up inspection of the fireplace.

If your night on the sofa is during a planned visit rather than an overnight stay born out of spontaneous necessity, your host might well have provided a pillow to make the experience as bed-like as possible. However, if you're merely staying on the premises because you got carried away with the tequila and are therefore wearing borrowed pyjamas and that kind of thing, such a vertebral aid as a pillow might have been forgotten. This presents a dilemma regarding the resting place for your head. I'm never sure if it's permissible in these circumstances to substitute the lounge cushions that are used by the family for their daytime lumbar padding. It seems innocent enough on the face of it, especially as a one-off, but then it would seem abhorrent to serve up the same unwashed pillowcase used by the last guest if the visitor were sleeping in a bed. To be safe, I have been known to clothe a cushion with my t-shirt. Doing this essentially creates an artificial torso, like a segment of a mannequin, which you can then use as a successful pillow. It is important to remember to undress the cushion the next morning because dressing the soft furnishings up suggests that you're either taking the piss or have been extremely lonely in the night.

Many of these woes are averted if you are sleeping on a sofa bed. A sofa bed is usually thoroughly comfortable and provides the opportunity for a late-night team-building exercise between you and your host as the two of you feebly attempt to make sense of the clips and folding legs that require both an engineering degree and a fluent command of Swedish to operate without serious injury. Several hours after embarking on this operation, you will have a very serviceable bed with perfectly adequate – generous, even – levels of space and comfort in which you can sleep for about forty-five minutes, after which time it is daylight again and time to start reassembling the thing before anyone can sit down.

I had a friend who purchased a sofa bed for her studio apartment, in which the living room moonlighted as the bedroom. She insisted that the bed would be neatly folded back to sofa mode each morning so that the space could revert to its daytime rôle as a reception room. I assured her, perhaps a touch indelicately, that she was talking bollocks. She would, I haughtily scoffed, convert it once – ever – and the conversion in question would be its first transition from sofa to bed. I was half right: she folded it back on the first morning with the assistance of a friend who happened to call in for coffee, whereupon it became apparent that it required two people and a socket set to change the position of the thing with any remote ease. She subsequently had to sleep on it in sofa mode for a week before a suitably muscular yet learned team was available to assist with converting it back again. After this, daytime guests were always received on the bed.

For some people, being encouraged to get comfortable atop someone's bed when merely popping round for a cup of tea or alternative beverage might feel like a faint line has been crossed or indeed like the acquaintance has been fast-tracked. However, in the case just outlined, the boundaries for me were rapidly and robustly reinforced when my glass of red wine somehow evacuated itself across the while pillowcases, causing them to resemble objects of critical forensic importance. Subsequent visits saw me being shown to a chair positioned in a wipe-clean exclusion zone, ostensibly because I might have enjoyed sitting beside the warm radiator. While a repeat invitation serves as the ultimate affirmation of your good conduct as a guest, it is also a boost to the ego to find that the furnishings haven't been covered with polythene sheeting when you make your second appearance.

ELEVEN

Bathroom Security

A man's bathroom is his castle, as the saying does not go, but any castle must anticipate an invasion. Two important lessons can be learned from using the bathroom facilities on someone else's premises: (1) that you should always use the WC before leaving your own home and (2) however much you believe yourself to be operating on your own terms in the solace of someone else's bathroom, your security could be compromised at any time.

The need to bear these pearls in mind was evident to me some years before I was a regular house guest myself. I used to live with someone who, not being one to jump to conclusions, had the curious habit of trying the bathroom door and redundantly inquiring 'Is someone in?' upon finding it locked. This was presumably to gain peace of mind that the sound of running water was coming from the shower and did not indicate a leaking roof. From the other side of the door and while completing intimate personal routines in a state of undress, it was difficult to compose a sincere response. If the audible water had indeed been pouring unbidden through the ceiling into an unoccupied yet locked bathroom, it would have relied on a previous occupant of the room having bolted themselves inside before exiting via the window and abseiling down the side of the house. The likelihood of such a sequence of events unfolding anywhere is remote, even to the most fanciful risk-assessor. My fellow resident eventually discerned a trend, where there was indeed someone attempting to relieve themselves or shower in fragmented peace on the other side of the door every single time he asked. Following this realisation, the question was changed to 'Who's in?' I'm not sure what effect this variable had on his subsequent plan of action or what else he planned to do with the information. However lowly or noble the station of the poor harassed bathroom occupant, the man on the landing still had no hope of accessing the bathroom and he would just have had to endure a few minutes' delay to his shaving regime. Such unsolicited interaction curtailed the sense of tranquil solitude that one sought from twenty minutes' confinement behind a locked door. Even with the locked door keeping the man at bay, it was impossible to feel at ease knowing that he was hovering around outside, either plotting to break the door down to access his moustache comb or merely taking an esoteric census of bathroom occupants.

More idiosyncratic still was the character only a few weeks ago in my workplace who, upon finding the toilet locked while I was busy with my ablutions within, knocked on the door. My thought processes immediately froze. This was new territory. What was expected of me? Was this someone wanting to *help* me? What was I supposed to say? 'Come in'? It was a bit like an offer of assistance with bag packing when buying five items at the supermarket. A thoughtful gesture indeed but there are times when many hands do not, in fact, make light work. In a lavatorial context, 'the fewer the merrier,' to invert another old saying, is emphatically the motto.

Fearing that I was now on the brink of an invasion while using the workplace WC, I considered my next move. I was momentarily tempted to answer the door with my trousers around my ankles while wearing the guardedly benign expression with which one might typically receive a cold caller on the front step, but felt that to do so would perhaps consolidate the canvassing zip-assistant's conviction that their support was called for. I considered the words of the Miranda Warning, even though no one was being arrested (yet), and upheld my right to remain silent.

On the other side of the door, and from the polar opposite point of view, it soon became apparent that the would-be penny spender had seen fit to resolve the situation as he had interpreted it by summoning a colleague known for his combination of practical aptitude and unassailable strength. This additional fellow tried the door handle with a devastatingly confident level of force before launching a full attack, all the while assuring his client that bodily comfort was mere moments away. The sound of splintering wood as the bolt was torn away from the doorframe, accompanied now by my vulnerable shrieks and protests as the gentlemen entered the room, confirmed that the door lock had been conquered along with the dignity of all concerned. My small party of visitors sheepishly retreated and I suspect we all contemplated handing in our notices.

Being targeted in this manner when locked inside a bathroom is off-putting enough, but at least one can dissuade the raiders or at least spend some seconds preparing for them if the door is already locked. This contrasts with the nerve-wracking threat of unimpeded visitors when one uses the facilities in a household that is short of a locking bathroom door. Such an omission could exist owing to an incomplete DIY project or a dysfunctional mechanism, or merely as a symptom of a close family unit. Whatever the circumstances, no anecdotal backstory provides reassurance to the occupant. I lived in a shared house with this shortcoming for a few years and it saw my housemates inadvertently get to know each other very well indeed, but guests were invariably unimpressed. Visitors staying the night and using the shower the next day were particularly allergic to the high likelihood of accidental intruders presenting themselves and it wasn't always much fun for outsiders to walk in on resident gentlemen draining their dragons. I eventually remembered to warn people of the defect and explained that a fully closed door signified an engaged facility. The residents having grown used to this primitive visual code, the lack of a lock never bothered anyone until a guest appeared and highlighted it via their unease. Sometimes we are so accustomed to inadequacy that we become blind to our own low standards.

A code system such as I describe can also have the bladder-stretching side effect of keeping people out of the bathroom under false pretences. If one's own bathroom boasts a locking door, or if one lives alone and can liberally engage in bodily relief with the door wide open, it is easy to overlook the need to restore the bathroom door to the official 'vacant' position. Someone not used to such a regime might absent-mindedly close the door behind them on exit and leave the impression that the facilities are still engaged.

The need for clarity in this department was made farcically apparent when I was invited to dine with the family of one of my piano pupils, who lived in a large and sprawling house near a pub. I ended up spending much of the time before lunch being treated – along with most of those living within the postal area – to an enforced recorder recital executed by one of the junior members of the family, in a distant room of the house. From the window of this room, I noticed several of the household's number cross the road and enter the pub in a shifty fashion. 'How utterly bizarre', I thought. The only explanation for everyone's sudden migration, it seemed to me, was that the pub was perhaps supplying food for my crafty hosts to pass off at table as their own, intimidated by the reputedly high culinary standards of the average penniless musician. Maybe I'm the only person ever to have attempted such a ruse and nobody else would dream of it, or indeed have any reason to. Anyway, I would have to play along and compliment their fine cooking, perhaps amusing myself by asking for the recipes, or indeed perhaps not as this would verge on biting – however playfully – the hand that was feeding me.

When we were all accounted for in the dining room while my ears continued to scream a ceaseless internal rendition of *Joe, Joe Stumped His Toe,* it transpired that those visiting the pub had been doing so to use the loo. I had unthinkingly closed the door behind me when vacating the house bathroom some hours earlier, thereby creating a false indication of occupation that had excluded the family members from their own toilet facility for most of the morning. It had been unanimously assumed that I had been in the bathroom for the duration. Goodness knows what they thought I had been getting up to in there, but the idea that I had willingly spent the entire time exposed to the shrill fortissimo of three recorder lessons' worth of amassed decibels was apparently too fantastic to be a credible account of my whereabouts. Everyone had underestimated the immunity that music teachers' nerves develop to such things. The music had rendered me unable to hear the murmurs of lavatory-themed confoundment coming from elsewhere in the house. Indeed, I was unable to hear any sound at all for some hours after the recorder had been laid to rest. Appearing at least mildly deranged as I unintentionally shouted over the church-bell-level ringing in my ears, I constructed a family-friendly way of asking why the fuck they hadn't paid a visit to the recorder chamber before commuting to a public establishment to urinate. It transpired that the family members were only just regaining the ability to hear each other speaking, following a life-threateningly strident *Three Blind Mice* marathon, and no one was in a place yet, emotionally or aurally, to revisit the music room.

There are some households in which one is light-heartedly encouraged to sing to signify that one is on the bog. However, a rendition at 3 AM of the *Hallelujah Chorus* delivered in the unbeatable tiled acoustics of the bathroom, some hours after agreeing to finish the bottle, would probably go down with other occupants of the premises like flatulence in an elevator. Such a performance could also cause those newly awoken to fear as to what accomplishment was being so rapturously celebrated in there. Other households might offer an actual sign to affix to the door or make otherwise visible, clarifying that no audience is welcome for the activity taking place beyond the threshold. One snag with this system is that you might forget to remove the sign after withdrawing from the room.

If you are staying in foreign parts, you must ensure that you understand the implications of all bathroom notices and that you make no assumptions. I make this point after being let in on a tale of an English fellow staying with his girlfriend's parents in the Czech Republic in the infancy of their relationship. A sign was hanging outside the bathroom door that said 'obsazený'. This is Czech for 'engaged' in the context of a WC but, regrettably, the guest injudiciously assumed that it simply meant 'bathroom'. Fuelled with misplaced confidence upon having identified the correct room, he boldly opened the door and closed it behind him while simultaneously disrobing his member, in that most time-efficient way of certain gentlemen. Turning around, he observed with a presumed jolt of consternation that he had presented himself – more of himself than was ever likely to be desirable – in front of his future father-in-law, who sat on the john with his trousers around his ankles while reading what appeared to be the Czech equivalent of *Hello!* There followed a tempestuous exchange in two languages whereby the father caught with his pants down (as they say, with what turns out to be good reason) fired bullets of verbal remorse while the guest stood and begged for pardon. Despite them being thoroughly ignorant of each other's mother tongues, no language barrier prevented comprehension of the sentiments traded. How jolly unfortunate that this linguistic sixth sense had been so inactive on the landing in the face of the 'obsazený' sign.

Idiosyncrasy continued to abound in the actions of both parties. The Czech man's reflex had been to hide his magazine instead of his genitalia, identifying his possession of the former as the more dishonourable exposé, while the guest inexplicably remained in the room to plead his case, the reverberating shock of the situation having seemingly deprived him of the use of his legs. Perhaps his legs couldn't hear his brain shouting 'run, twat!' over the top of the bilingual turmoil. It later transpired that the father-in-law-to-be was the only member of his family who didn't realise that his vice of repairing to the bathroom for a presumed clandestine study of this publication was common knowledge. Father and son-in-law-to-be had now both viewed other things in there that they wished to keep confidential. Going from nought to sixty with such alacrity on the bonding front during the first visit cannot have spared a great deal of potential for deepening the acquaintance yet further on the second.

Despite the potential malfunctions, those staying where there's an established code of practice for bathroom privacy are substantially better off than where everything is left to chance. Things can be a bit edgier when staying with, for instance, someone who lives alone without the need of a methodology to prevent indignity and who thus forgets that the unsealable bathroom door could be a source of disquiet. There are many possible settings and circumstances where one might end up improvising a crude or comically feeble solution. A while ago, I experienced the once-(if-that)-in-a-lifetime treat of a weekend staying with a male voice choir in a convent. The convent was home to an abundance of nuns who seemed jolly excited to have an influx of strapping alpha males resident on the premises. I discovered during the first morning's shower that the door of the communal bathroom was entirely unfastenable, almost as if modifications had been hastily effected in advance of the laddish choir's arrival. Not in the mood to offer naked hospitality to disorientated or opportunistic religious en route to Mass or indeed to any gentlemen seeking a pre-breakfast dress rehearsal of *Singing in the Rain*, I gathered together the motley assortment of furniture that had bizarrely been abandoned in the room and used it to create a mighty fortress across the door to keep visitors at bay. I dauntlessly hosed myself down like the king of my castle for about half a minute until a pyjama-clad baritone carrying a towel, undeterred by the sound of running water, attempted to enter and join me. My tower of chairs and stools transpired to be as movable as the door itself and free-fell like a Jenga tower, with such percussion as to summon investigative nuns from the chapel. This left me centre-stage in my lathery bareness, provoking both the baritone and me to emit notes some distance beyond the range of the average soprano. We have not exchanged eye contact since.

A similarly compromising state of affairs prevailed in a house in which I once stayed in Paris, a rustic seven-bedroom edifice with an old key in the door of every room. Turning the bathroom door's rusty key produced much resistance and a cautionary grinding sound, warning me that I could expect to live out the rest of my days in the facility if I set about the delicate technology too brusquely. Some days into my stay, someone did just that and the key snapped. It's amazing how normal barricading oneself into a French bathroom with scales and a full pedal bin pushed up against the door feels after a couple of weeks, to the point where my instincts automatically continued the practice for several days when I got home.

Sometimes, the size and geography of the bathroom can affect the extent to which your pride can be damaged in the event of an invasion. In a small cloakroom, one can theoretically grab the door in an emergency to prevent trespassers from advancing further. However, I felt ill at ease during a recent stay in a house with a non-locking bathroom that was the size of the average suburban post office and in which the toilet faced the door. What on earth would happen here? I strategized that if I were busy on the bog and someone attempted to join me, I could have jumped up and attempted to slam the door in their face, but so large was the bathroom that this would merely have seen me running towards the sightseer with my pants down before meeting them in the middle of the room. The episode would perhaps have climaxed with an eccentric hug or a surprise handshake that could have featured forbidden and unruly additional appendages, somewhat subverting a romantic film cliché where the two parties are clothed and running across a beach at sunset instead of a linoleum floor. Perhaps the best thing would have been to have surrendered. I should have stayed seated, welcomed the visitor to the arena with a resigned grin and then quietly packed my bags and left forever.

A final warning in this department: if your host tells you not to lock the bathroom door because the lock has become impossible to unfasten, take them at their word. Make a mental note in size-seventy-two letters, bold and underlined. Your host will have lived with the system long enough to know to keep out if they find the door closed and you will ideally have followed whatever bit of protocol is required to keep intruders at bay. It does not pay to assume that any talent you may have for handiwork has bestowed you with an immunity to or a superior knowledge of the foibles of someone else's door lock, or indeed has automatically armed you to overcome the entrapping defects of which you were warned. If you forget, even after having flipped over a sign saying 'occupied' or whatever and then instinctively lock the door once you're inside via force of habit, your memory will certainly be jogged when you find yourself imprisoned behind said door at 3 AM and have to curl up for the rest of the night in the bath.

TWELVE

Animals: Before Bed

A little while ago, I experienced a sense of foreboding upon arriving at a friend's house for morning coffee. This was on account of some unsettling enquiries that this friend had made the night before while assessing my chances of survival on his premises, specifically whether or not I was 'alright with dogs' and whether or not I had a peanut allergy. These questions would not have seemed too strange in isolation from one another but it seemed a little offbeat for them to be presented as two halves of the same whole. I am in fact allergic to peanuts but had submitted an instant and unconditional 'yes' in answer to the dog question. I had also subsequently asked about the connection between the two particulars.

'Oh, well, my dog reacts quite violently to new people,' he explained with pragmatic understatement. 'He has a rubber toy that I can fill with peanut butter to distract him so that he doesn't eat you.' My 'yes' was now clouded with a shade of 'no' as I attempted to compose a diplomatic way of suggesting we met at a cafe instead. I had been naïve to the implications of his concerns. I should have had a caveat along the lines of 'so long as they're not satanic killers that want to rip me apart' appended to my response. Moreover, my peanut allergy now weakened my ability to defend myself with what was seemingly the only weapon against this crazed monster. However, since my allergy is fairly mild and only really causes me any chunderous bother if I actually eat a peanut, I keenly encouraged my friend to press ahead with Operation Buttery Chew Toy if it was the only prayer of resistance against a savage attack. In the event, the hound was banished to an upstairs room – with said peanut-butter-charged plaything – while I stood and trembled pathetically on the periphery of the situation, hoping that the plywood door keeping the animal at bay would prove to be a sufficiently fang-proof barrier.

This potentially flesh-threatening scenario brought home to me that a visit to someone's home can be a significantly more hair-raising business when the host happens to own a creature that is exceptionally ferocious or simply of a breed of which you suffer a phobia. It is especially profound for all concerned when you have not been briefed regarding the beast that could greet you on arrival. The first sign of an undisclosed pet might be when your ringing of the doorbell immediately triggers a spine-chilling airing of carnivorous aggression within. Your heart may then drop, race, or both. Your host opens the door and the animal continues to express itself, now in a more intimate and acutely tactile manner with this wooden barrier removed and almost certainly on your side of the threshold. If it is a life form towards which you bear – and I shall spare you all attempts to craft the potential second-rate pun lurking there – a touch of apprehension, you might now be clenching for England (or whichever nation you hold most dear and would wish to represent via your buttocks) while attempting to appear tolerant of or even pleasantly surprised by the encounter.

Your posture will become feebly defensive and your voice's pitch might rise an octave or two beyond its usual register as you attempt some sort of anxious small talk with the pet or helplessly try to repel its advances.

Animal owners respond to this scenario in different ways. Whatever the approach used, their standard opener to the mediation process is '[s]he's very friendly'. Many pet owners will automatically leap to your aid and admonish their animals to detach themselves from you or, in more memorable cases, plead with them to put you back down on the ground. This is even if you're actually quite content with the interaction. Other hosts, especially those who have shared their houses with such creatures all their lives, might still intervene but with less urgency. You might be struck by how their relatively conservative response offers a fascinating contrast with the intensifying tetchiness you are now feeling as the beast heartily snacks on your shins. As you meditate on this disparity and perhaps struggle to mask the entirety of your apprehension, the animal's owner might now drily say 'Oh, sorry. I should have checked – are you not good with snow leopards?' or whatever it may happen to be.

If it is a dog that receives you on arrival, there is a variety of forms that its welcome to you can take. If you are fundamentally intimidated by dogs, you will likely interpret all their advances as attempts to maim you. If the dog bares its teeth or proceeds to sink them into your ankle in a spiteful or hungry manner, your judgement might not be so irrational. The hound might alternatively jump up in a curious or friendly fashion, lick you to an inescapable extent or, perhaps most outlandishly if you are not used to the peculiarities of dogs, attempt to have sex with you.

I first had the dubious honour of this latter phenomenon during adolescence when I was staying with a friend and found myself incompetently grappling with the fitting of a duvet cover, which I inevitably ended up wearing at one point in my unmethodical efforts to make the bed. The dog seemingly thought that lilac was my colour and promptly saw me in a new light. 'He's saying that he *really* likes you,' annotated my friend, drawing mirth from my naïve bemusement as the terrier urgently thrust back and forth while adhered to my leg. More recently, after a comparable incident left me intrigued by the canine thought process that prompts such intemperate expressions of intimacy at moments when a polite paw-shake would be sufficient, I conducted some research. This involved entering search terms into my browser of a nature that would have been incommodious to justify to third parties. One article on a site called *Daily Puppy* clarified that 'while dogs don't hump humans to try and mate with them, they may do it as a means of masturbation'. Well, that's comforting I suppose. You could be insulted that you are being objectified so and that the affection is being offered on such a superficial, disposable and emotionally disconnected basis, but at least the pooch isn't trying to force you into anything serious before you've had the opportunity to assess your longer-term compatibility.

Staying in a house with animals can also offer an eye-opening social tourism excursion. I must clarify at this point that I am perfectly fond of animals. I enjoy the comforting, cosy novelty of a cat curled up on my knee and the relief when its claws have stopped puncturing my clothing and skin. I similarly enjoy the company of dogs that don't look at me like I'm prey. Moreover, I fully appreciate how much pets mean to families but, not being an animal owner myself, I sometimes underestimate the extent to which a lot of pets are pampered and humanised. The greatest challenge at this point can lie simply in keeping one's mouth shut.

I remember once finding it slightly eccentric when a dog was included as an equal party in an order over the phone to a fish-and-chip shop, particularly when the hound then sat at the table and ate his cod and chips from a plate identical to that of everyone else. I was stranded entirely alone on my island of bemusement. As we sat down to eat, I wryly commented that I was looking forward to watching the dog using a knife and fork, prompting solemn elucidation from all sides of the table about how he didn't use a knife and fork because he was a dog and it would be difficult for him. 'In fact,' declared the dog's owner in termination of my ludicrous line of inquiry, 'it would be *almost* impossible.' It was interesting to see where the line of reason was drawn. People exchanged glances acknowledging my low intelligence. Fortunately for all concerned, I had enough about me to realise that responding *'almost?!'* in a tone verging on insincere would isolate me further in what was already a rather lonely position.

Further examples of this parallel mentality, where the hand of equality with humans is extended to pets, are manifested in the homes of many animal owners. A friend recently reported having observed via a wide-open bedroom door that a flight of plush and fluffy 'cat stairs' was installed at the foot of his host's bed. People reading this who do not have cat stairs fitted to their beds will not require me to say anything more, while those who *do* have cat stairs will wonder why I'm mentioning it at all.

Adding to the business of animals in bedrooms, there are many pet owners who, particularly if the children have left home, devote a bedroom to the creature and refer to it as 'Roger's room,' or whatever, when Roger is not a human but a cocker spaniel or a goose. If his is the only bedroom in the house not allocated to a person, Roger may end up evicted from his room in order for you to sleep therein. Roger will likely be held in higher esteem than most homo sapiens by his owners, who may have sucked air through their teeth over the phone about the feasibility of your being welcome to stay the night on the premises at all. I was once told I couldn't stay with someone because they only had two bedrooms: 'One's ours and one's Rupert's.' Rupert was a Persian cat and his room contained a sumptuous double bed. Admittedly, there exists the unflattering possibility that these people didn't have a skewed perspective regarding their feline's domestic requirements and merely wished to keep me away. They may have received character references that warned of my propensity to make asinine suggestions at the dinner table regarding animals' use of cutlery. That said, the notion of the cat needing to luxuriate each night in a bedroom measuring twenty square metres to get a full eight hours, combined with the deadpan sincerity with which the information was presented, did not come across as a lifestyle choice that was being improvisationally fabricated as a cover story. Even if a host is happy to give the go-ahead, it is sometimes not without making sure you understand the hardship you have inflicted upon the household's four-or-however-many-legged inhabitant.

If there are pets on the premises, your host may have issued you with guidelines about closing doors during your stay, or indeed about leaving them open. This is often to stop the animals from doing inherently destructive things in accordance with their instincts, such as eating the coffee table. It goes down well if you bear these policies in mind from the beginning of your stay. Having been given no instructions, I once left a door open and – well, you probably guessed – half an hour later, my friend's house rabbit had all but gobbled up a pair of knickers that had been suspended from the clothes horse. It was one of those classic instalments of misfortune that anyone other than me would have seen coming a mile off. Indeed, this was the implication when I was then given a stern but hopelessly retrospective talking-to about the need to keep the doors closed. A somewhat more poignant state of affairs is when an elderly cat lives on the premises and, upon being accidentally shut inside a room for too long, lacks the bladder control to avoid moistening the soft furnishings. It is in everyone's interests for the cat not to relieve itself on the sofa, and certainly in your own interests for it not to have the opportunity to urinate on your bed.

An even more potentially farcical scenario is when a property is home to an entire food chain. This necessitates meticulously secured physical barriers to prevent the entire menagerie from devouring itself, with each creature ending up inside another like a set of carnivorous Russian dolls.

When you go to bed, you might be resigned to the inevitability that animals will enter the room during your occupation of it. It is therefore advisable to animal-proof your belongings as far as possible. I have yet to meet a cat or dog that can unzip a suitcase (although they probably exist) and so sealing your things into there before going to bed can help with security. Lots of animals enjoy emptying bags, boxes and drawers and then hiding or adorably mutilating the contents. Cats may enter the room in small teams and search your bags to check that you haven't opportunistically stashed away the family barometer. I was once at a social gathering in a colleague's house when a ginger cat suspended the polite conversation by appearing in the middle of the living room carrying one of the host's bras, having presumably hauled it down from upstairs. This provoked mirth on the part of all but the host herself, who jumped up and wrestled the sturdy hoist from the animal. She then protested, most unconvincingly, that it was 'just a scarf'. If that had been true, it was quite the most complex scarf I had ever seen – not in pattern or colour, for it was merely plain white, but in shape and structure. Most of it didn't look like it would offer much insulation, but hats off (and hats only) nonetheless to the ingenious designer who filled the gap in the market for an item of winter clothing that could safely carry two family-size Christmas puddings for consumption on the hoof without spilling any of the cream.

It is not merely out of being precious about one's possessions that it is prudent to keep things out of the reach of curious animals. That chocolate is a deadly substance to dogs is a fact well known by everyone apart from the dogs themselves and they do rather like to avail themselves of any they find lying around. If you have purchased any quantity of chocolate for a loved one as a souvenir of your trip, or indeed if you just have it in your suitcase for reasons that you don't need to justify to anyone, it will be infinitely less hassle for all concerned if you make a special effort to make it inaccessible. You won't lose your chocolate and it is commonly held that the overnight stays in which the friendship remains as buoyant on departure as it was on arrival are the ones where the host isn't left burying a family pet.

THIRTEEN

Going to the Lavatory During the Night

I have been told that my fearful anticipation of the following scenario is a trifle irrational but it is nonetheless one of my worst nightmares. Upon nature calling during the night while I am staying with a friend or relative, I will get out of bed to embark on a stealthy safari to the facilities. I will go to great pains not to wake anyone, via careful management of my footsteps, the doors and the lighting. Once safely locked inside the bathroom, I will stand and gingerly relieve myself. Upon having done so, and this is where I am perhaps being a touch over-imaginative, I will turn around to behold the surreal sight of my host sitting silently in the bath. They are, at least in my neurotic conjecture, upright but motionless with a neutral, slightly vacant expression, blinking less than one might in less disturbing circumstances and possibly holding a glass of wine. It is 3 AM or thereabouts and so, up until my entering the room and switching on the light, they would presumably have been bathing in the dark. Neither of us will say anything. I will wash my hands – because of course remaining in the room instead of jumping out of the window into the traffic below is the reasoned course of action at this point – and then nonchalantly take leave. In the morning, as for the rest of time, there will be no mention of the incident and my host's temperament and eyelid movement will be entirely normal once again.

Accessing the bathroom during the night is a pertinent issue for me, not so much because I frequently wake up with a need to do so but because I am something of a night owl and so often end up completing my teeth-brushing regime an hour or two after my host has retired. I am therefore still active after the point at which friends have become strangers until the morning's alarm call. If the evening has been called to a close at 11 PM, for instance, I might well remain awake reading, dealing with Emails or flicking through everyone's carefully curated self-portraits on social media until 1 AM or so. Only then, by which time I am usually responsible for the only light still on in the street, does it occur to me that I ought to be winding down.

Although a materialisation of my chilling bathroom rendezvous scenario is somewhat remote in likelihood, the anxiety leading to its fabrication is not unfounded. I believe it was triggered some time ago when staying with an old friend in London. We arrived back at his stylish pad at 10:30 PM. His fiancé, who at the time I had not yet met, was already asleep on the other side of a closed door. My friend briefed me on the essentials, commencing with a gesture towards an assortment of soft furnishings graciously laid on for my comfort, continuing through such customary things as the aforementioned Wi-Fi password and concluding with a tutorial – delivered with feeling – about how to flush the toilet so that the fire brigade would not need to be summoned during the night to drain the apartment. He then bade me goodnight and left me to grow orientated with the foreign land that was his living room. My brain, being a product of northern England, was still stimulated by the frippery of being in London as I took in what would be my surroundings for the next seven hours. I put the array of pillows and blankets into an effective order and spent some time reading. No risk assessment could have saved me from the tit I was about to make of myself.

I felt the pressure. My oldest friend's partner had allowed me into her home based solely on a character reference from her other half. She had been trusting of me with her living space and hadn't felt the need to interview me before allowing me into it, although perhaps this was her way of delaying meeting a bumbling eccentric like me until morning. Determined not to make a nuisance of myself, I tottered falteringly across the pitch-dark hallway to the bathroom and carefully selected the correct door, adjacent to the bedroom of my comatose hosts. I then entered the bathroom, wincing as the door hinge rotated with a high-pitched glissando that sliced through the night like a wolf howling at the Moon. I was determined not to generate any more noise and so, once I was safely on the other side of the door, I painstakingly guided its bolt into the hole.

The quietest possible click confirmed that my journey was complete. My destination was reached. I had secured myself into this palace of personal procedure and could now strut around freely. There was nothing to restrain me from removing all my clothes or performing a handstand for no reason at all, had I been someone who could attempt a handstand without needing urgent surgery afterwards. I had enclosed myself into perfect darkness, having overlooked a light switch that I now realised was outside the door but, no matter, my phone torch radiated the brightness required to illuminate my ablutions. I exhaled gladly and celebrated having crossed the finish line by brazenly unzipping my flies in anticipation of bodily relief.

Turning around, I now met with a reality that caused me immediate and severe palpitations: the bathroom had a second door – devastatingly wide-open – that led straight into my hosts' bedroom. Far from the confined sanctuary that I thought I had attained, I was in fact standing as good as rod-in-hand at the foot of my friend's bed in the middle of the night while holding a torch. The precision and delicacy that had characterised the operation up until this point were abandoned at once. My balls hit the ceiling. I grabbed the open door and slammed it shut with a report loud enough to suggest that I was altering the fittings with a weighty mallet. I didn't break the fourth wall by looking any distance through the sea of darkness into the audience. This had not been an interactive piece of showmanship thus far and I had no wish for it to become one. I imagined the two of them having been lying bemusedly in bed, possibly even hiding under the covers in grim anticipation, while their bathroom transformed beyond their control into the stage on which I performed this extremely niche piece of theatre. It would have been an eccentric spectacle indeed: one man entering on tiptoes stage-right by torchlight, executing the most painfully studious exhibition of door-closing the world had ever seen and concluding his show by dropping his kecks, the latter presumably in lieu of taking a bow. In any case, no applause was forthcoming and indeed no feedback was offered in the morning. My friendship with one of the bedroom's occupants was in its twentieth year at this point but, to his beloved, I had potentially just made my first impression.

Avoiding Detection in the Face of Unjust Factors

The sense of being in the spotlight when making a night-time journey across a landing is never so heightened as when other occupants of the house decide to sleep with their bedroom doors open, not giving you so much as a chance to avoid disturbing them.

Why on earth do people do this? They deserve to be woken up. The bedroom door is the very thing – the *only* thing – that provides a screen between your nocturnal maladroit and the sleeping lion on the other side. When this barrier is not sonically watertight, your host is effectively setting you up to make a nuisance of yourself. When the bedroom doors are closed you are, at worst, an abstract soundtrack. Many potential faux pas are obscured from the record and, when tiptoeing around with minimal light for orientation, you can at least take your time without feeling any audience pressure. With someone in bed on the other side of an open door, however, it all feels a bit more exposed.

From the moment you exit your room, you are self-consciously in no-man's-land. You summon the courage to push yourself away from the jetty that is your bedroom, nervously emerging onto the landing like a duckling being introduced to the water. You then commence a ponderous hopscotch to your destination across alternately creaky floorboards. The person on the other side of the open door might be ambiguously silent. Alternatively, they might have transformed into a human orchestra performing an involuntary symphony of comatose bodily sounds. There might be steady snoring in the bassoon section and glissandos of heavy breathing from the cellos. Your host might even be talking in his or her sleep, potentially revealing scandalous information. While this cacophony might provide some reassurance that your host is asleep, any variation in the tempo or rhythm is your first and only warning that, with one moment of clumsiness on your part, they could wake up in a matter of seconds and eat you. If the bodily music stops, you're for it. Your heart now pounding, it matters more than ever in this scenario that your transition to the bathroom is smooth and efficient.

The host who sleeps with the door open will typically adorn their landing with tall and unstable vases, strategically placing them on your flight path. It is prudent on the one hand to carry a torch to limit the possibility of colliding with such breakables, along with any houseplants, cats or bookshelves that might also lie in the way but, on the other hand, the light from such a device might immediately find its way through the open bedroom door and threaten the occupant's repose. If there's the possibility of your host being awake and able to see you, it could add a dose of sass if you don a balaclava before passing their bedroom door on your torch-lit mission to the bathroom.

Aside from the fundamental business of waking people up, if the host has an open-door policy for their bedroom door there can be an uneasy feeling of one's every nocturnal move being registered. Your conduct is being silently assessed. Notes are being taken. One feels the need to pass doorways delicately but efficiently. Too slow a crossing could suggest you're doing something more sinister out there. There is a sense of needing to operate discreetly in the bathroom, sparing listeners any particularly poignant sound effects, and not to take too long. Your host cannot see what you're doing in there, thank the Lord, but it is not good to provide their imagination with the opportunity to fill the blanks.

Once you get back into bed, you might think you are immune from blotting your proverbial copybook any further. However, this fails to be the case if you then hear the tediously unmistakable sound of a tap dripping in the bathroom that you have just vacated. If you can hear it, it is safe to assume that whoever lies behind the open door can hear it too. The sound is percussive and persistent and distracting. If you have been dealt a similar hand in life to me, this trickling time bomb will be counting down in a household that is as piously devoted to the environment as it is to frugality. The house will have solar panels fitted. Mealtimes will be dominated by conversations about supermarket special offers and the family compost heap. Leaving a tap dripping on these premises will be no less offensive than pouring a bottle of the best wine down the sink in the name of empty-headed banter.

What should you do in this situation? You might fear being presented with an invoice over breakfast for the escaped water. Should you get up to turn the tap off? That could cause a further disturbance. What if they can't actually hear the tap dripping but *can* hear you having two bathroom trips within five minutes? They might even storm out of bed and switch the tap off themselves. Imagine having to meet them at breakfast the next morning after such a fiasco. The ideal resolution to all this comes along when the agony of the decision and the weighing up of the complex minutiae eventually bores you into a deep sleep.

The Flushing Dilemma

A similar minefield is the night-time toilet-flushing policy. This is something else that you bitterly come to realise was omitted from the bedtime information presentation.

You wouldn't remotely go leaving the yellow to mellow, as they (although I'm not sure who) say, during the day. Flushing at night, however, is another potential cause of sound pollution, to be weighed up against the visual and olfactory pollution that could greet the next person to use the bathroom if you decide against pushing the button. In addition to being a dilemma with the potential to divide hosts and guests, this matter also causes disharmony between household members.

So high do passions run where twilight toilet-flushing is concerned that many have taken to the public domain to air their views. 'My ex-husband was a non-flusher and I found it gross!' shares a lady on one internet board, not confirming whether or not this is the reason for the 'ex' status. Another contributor speaks of having known an 'intelligent' couple who smugly rejoiced in drinking many gallons of water each day so that their urine would be diluted to a point where the toilet seldom needed to be flushed at any hour of the day or night. Presumably, this couple were unable to take to the proverbial airwaves to tell their story themselves, owing to their curious policy rendering them unable to leave the bathroom for long enough to fire up the computer. Her Late Majesty the Queen was on the throne for over seventy years and it sounds like a similar – although less prestigious – fate might have been in store for this twosome.

Weighing up the pros and cons, it is probably best to flush. Although this carries the aforementioned risk of tearing people from slumber and turning them into resentful passengers on your journey of waste elimination, your movements might already be on the radar anyway. The host with the open door may well have registered that you are on the john. They might be expecting – *waiting* even – for you to flush. They might be incapable of getting back to sleep if you don't. A lamentable judgement of your character might form if you audibly fail to flush, exacerbated by the judge's grim fear of what you might have left behind. In an extreme case, you might return to your room and then hear your host immediately get up to expel your bodily deposits. You would be unable to face them ever again* and would need to leave before sunrise via the bedroom window. In any case, waking someone up with the sound of a torrent of clean water is a less humbling state of affairs than their finding your maturing sample in the bowl the next morning.

Let There Be Light

Some unexpected turmoil at the end of the journey to the bathroom might present itself when you are working out how to switch on the light. Bathroom light switches come in two main guises: a cord suspended from the bathroom ceiling, or a switch outside the door. The cords are frequently adjacent to and indistinguishable from cords that may activate such noisier alternatives as fans if indeed these do not automatically come on with the light. Cords are frequently anchored by substantial lumps of wood or metal that smash against the wall on release. Someone with whom I recently stayed had cutely hung a heart-shaped piece of slate next to the metal pull cord, presumably because the metal merely striking the bare wall at 2 AM wasn't considered sufficiently noisy.

Sometimes, presumably for highly technical reasons that only a rogue electrician would understand, bathroom light switches outside the door can be strategically placed

---

*   I refer here to your host and not your bodily deposits, although I
suppose the latter would also be true.

next to buttons with other critical functions, some of which are highly incompatible with a discreet night-time toilet trip. They can also be adjacent to switches for other nearby lights. Where this is the case, it's not always easy to distinguish between the one that will illuminate your road to an empty bladder from the one that will flood your host's bedroom with light through their irksomely ajar door. Of course, if you haven't had the appropriately neurotic level of foresight to have closed the bathroom door before switching on the light, such a blaze of brightness will result in any case.

I once stayed in a house that sported burglar alarm controls next to the bathroom door, inviting the unbriefed, unsuspecting and half-asleep to fumble around in their vicinity while aiming for the bathroom light. To be fair, the bathroom lock was broken and so activating the burglar alarm would, however bluntly, have put out a message to the inhabitants of the house (and the street) that the facility were engaged.

Sometimes the wrong button gets pressed on purpose. We've all had the droll experience of being mid-flow in a windowless toilet facility, only for someone to turn off the light under an illusion of their possessing unrivalled comic prowess. Those on the receiving end of such a wheeze can experience a sense of strandedness and a loss of control. Indeed, for those standing up to get the job done, it can cause a devastating breakdown in accuracy. The startling darkness can occasion one to hose the place down in the manner of an elephant that has lost command of its trunk. This is typically followed, from the other side of the door, by either a profuse apology (in very rare cases), a trill of mirth or a deadpan silence while the distinguished intellectual who blatantly did it tweely feigns being in a different part of the house. Having said all this, it would be very distasteful indeed if someone were to commit such a deliberate and dastardly act against you in the middle of the night. Were they to do so, you would be justified in subverting all social protocol for the remainder of your stay.

Some houses have the toilet in a separate chamber from the bathroom, which means that, if you're going full-hygiene, you will be required to do two lots of faffing around with doors and light switches. This could potentially see you staggering past multiple open bedroom doors and terminating more ornaments than you might have done otherwise. These layouts tend to be in older houses, which might also have quaint doorknobs that make a loud crash when you let go of them. The same houses might also boast a cheeky step down into the bathroom so that, to your surprise, you plunge toe-first into the facility and let out a startled yelp. In this sort of setup, especially if the two stations of porcelain are a long way apart, you may end up creating such a disturbance that you may as well make a night of it. If you happen to have a bugle with you, take it out and play *The Last Post*.

Visiting the Neighbours

One of the classic anxieties of going walkabout on someone else's landing in the middle of the night is the possibility of accidentally returning to the wrong room. Somehow, the number of doors on a landing seems to multiply after dark and they all look the same. Moreover, one's heightened efforts to be discreet can impair one's geographical awareness.

There are various extents to which returning to the wrong room is a problem. If you accidentally open the wrong door, barely enter (admittedly preferable to entering barely) and then withdraw upon realising your mistake, all is easily forgiven and indeed might go unnoticed if your host is asleep and you manage not to disturb them. However, a slightly lengthier breakfast-time discussion might follow an attempt – however unwitting – to climb into someone else's bed. The outcome of said discussion could range from a permanent ban from the premises to an invitation to move in.

It isn't essential to have even made it to bed before one's aptitude for causing botheration in this manner can be activated. I realised this one evening on the Parisian premises with the broken bathroom key featured in Chapter Eleven. I arrived back there at midnight. The old house was in darkness and its occupants were asleep. I tiptoed up the wooden stairs to my room, closed the door behind me with minimal percussion, turned on the light and put down my bag. Upon turning around, I discovered that my room had been redecorated, enlarged and had had new windows fitted in my few hours' absence. More arrestingly still, my host, a local councillor no less, had evidently decided that she and her husband should use my bed as the platform for conceiving their next child. It suddenly struck home with life-threatening clarity that the house had three storeys and I had not climbed as many stairs as I ought to have done. I was suddenly failed as miserably by my command of the French language as the gentleman was failed by his attempts to shield his dignity with the duvet.

I have often stayed with friends living in house-share situations where all but one of the people in the house are strangers to me. While you might not be a personal guest to the residents with whom you are unacquainted, they are silent partners in the hosting agreement and so are to be taken very much into account. Night-time errors can compromise things severely when someone with whom you have no bond is affected by your blundering. Having perhaps been supplied with only the sketchiest biographical information relating to you, a stranger might not necessarily know that your inadvertent appearance at their bedside, caused by your taking a wrong turn at 4 AM, is an accident. If they haven't even met you before bedtime, they also probably won't process that you're not a burglar. The notable exception was an acquaintance who erroneously inserted himself into his friend's female housemate's room late one night and, despite apologising profusely, wasn't hurried out until the next morning. Indeed, he proceeded to visit the same room by invitation several nights a week for the following six months, doubtlessly inserting himself on those occasions as well. A lucky boy indeed, although a rare outcome and the odds of chancing upon such nocturnal hospitality are too poor for me to recommend such an approach in good conscience as an alternative to *Tinder*.

Of course, you could alternatively – or additionally – find yourself on the receiving end of an error of this kind. If another guest is staying in another room on the premises, they too could find themselves disorientated en route back to their room and end up paying *you* an accidental visit. If you're the sort of person who's instinctively likely to wallop a robber with a blunt instrument, it's perhaps advisable while on location to hold your horses for a few seconds until the intruder's face has come into focus, just to ensure that they are not merely a washed-up temporary resident. Committing grievous bodily harm towards your co-habitants, however well-intentioned, can sour things for everyone.

It is very rare for one to be expected to walk through the bedrooms of sleeping hosts for any reason but it is not unheard of. Earlier, I mentioned the night when I was unable to urinate until morning owing to the only bathroom being an en-suite to the sleeping quarters of my host and his partner. This was in contrast to my friend's recent stay in a rambling Victorian terraced house beset by a miserable litany of malfunctioning commodities. The facilities in the communal bathroom were in so poor a state of repair, or so the lonely host claimed, that my friend was invited to use the master bedroom's en-suite. He would therefore walk freely through the proprietor's bedroom each time he needed a wash or a wee. My friend disciplined his bladder so as to avoid a night-time expedition through the inner sanctum but he wished to shower on the morning of departure before catching an early train. The sun had not yet risen. He gingerly opened the heavy oak door to his host's bedroom and crept inside in a dainty manner. Such a controlled disposition was difficult to maintain upon the discovery of the room's occupant enjoying sound repose while starfishing atop the opulent velvet bedding in a condition that could most faithfully have been described as 'bollock naked'.

Having obtained relief in the bathroom, you might well feel relief of a different variety when you finally make it back to your sleeping quarters. It is certainly advisable that you don't get these two types of relief the wrong way round. You can now relax, but it's still perhaps best not to forget where you are.

FOURTEEN

Other Ways of Making a Cacophonous Nuisance of Oneself

It is not just by going to the bathroom – or indeed setting off to go anywhere – that you can be a source of night-time commotion. It seems that there are plenty of ways in which one can paint oneself as a rowdy arsehole from the seclusion of one's bedroom. This is the case whether the room adjoins that of the host, is distanced from the host's quarters by a vast landing or is even on a different storey.

It is easy to think, once you are sealed inside your designated space for the night, that you are as inaudible as you are invisible. However, that is rather like assuming that your indelicate remarks about someone standing two metres away cannot be heard by them because you are facing the other way or are on the other side of a closed door. On numerous occasions, I have been within earshot of profound insights regarding my shortcomings, as a result of the false sense of security offered by plywood doors giving pontificating mouths the boldness to express themselves at full volume and with cold-blooded frankness. Without these flimsy sound barriers creating an illusion of confidentiality for the acidic, I would probably never have been party to such morale-boosting observations as the resemblance one of my previous haircuts apparently bore to a toilet brush. However soundproof your surroundings may appear, therefore, it is usually best to monitor your volume with the sort of healthy paranoia that accompanies the most jovial social occasions.

Having successfully negotiated creaky floorboards and managed to be light-of-foot en route to and from the bathroom, the relief of having docked in your bedroom after a tumultuous landing-crossing might make you feel like you can strut around like you're in an isolated castle, separated from your cohabitants by a moat and a thousand acres. Not so. This was once made clear to me when staying in a friend's attic room. Before being alone in the room, I had endured several minutes of intense self-consciousness when making my way up to my designated storey. The narrow wooden staircase appeared to have been specially engineered both to amplify one's footsteps tenfold and to warn slumbering householders to get to a place of safety before their guest came crashing through the ceiling. I assumed that those resident on the premises were immune to these unmuffled thuds and groans, but I was still mightily relieved when I had made it to the summit and was no longer the cause of them.

My kind and generous hosts had turned in, it being after midnight, but I had a great deal of packing to do for my return journey so made a start on this. With the bedroom door now closed, I could potter around to my heart's content without disturbing a soul. Indeed, I could have got cracking with some joinery or held an all-night Lindy Hop function. At the very least, I could sort myself the most strategically packed suitcase of my adult life without the hindrance of needing to consider my decibel level.

After a little while, I heard someone ascending the creaky stairs to my level. I opened the door in response to my host's somewhat agitated stage whisper of my name, affording her a panoramic view of how I had desecrated the room with my belongings, and she pleaded with me in her night attire to go to bed because the sound of my walking around on the venerable floorboards was keeping her awake and she had to be up early for work. I have seldom felt so immediately repentant. Blissful ignorance turned to acute self-awareness. I realised at once that I was being a tool, incompatible with other humans. A *decibellend*, one could say. I had just naïvely assumed that, since I was on a different storey, my movements were off the radar. This misjudgement had combined with a fleeting forgetfulness that I live in my own time zone. It was the fact that she felt she had to justify herself to me with her need to be up early that made me feel particularly contrite. She would have been quite within her rights to have told me that I was a nocturnal imbecile and to have left the matter there. In fairness (sort of), the fine whisky with which her husband had plied me an hour earlier had perhaps impaired both my introspection and my daintiness but I felt this line of vindication wasn't a good one to pursue when the only possible outcome could have been a no-whisky-for-Matthew policy thereafter. It seemed only reasonable to set my alarm for an excessively early time the next morning so that I had had no more sleep than anyone else.

While creaky floorboards are a fairly mainstream hurdle, other potential challenges are more novel. I shared a flat in Paris for a few weeks with a girl who was charming but a maddeningly light sleeper, to the point of almost total unsuitability for co-existence with others

– or maybe just with me. Either way, perhaps because she was French and we were in her country, it went without saying that my life would have to be rearranged to accommodate her ability to be awoken by a field mouse potentially breaking wind three streets away. At the end of our first week under the same roof, we coincided in the kitchen one evening and, after an affable exchange of uncontroversial highlights from our respective days, she hit me – thankfully not literally – with a list of ways in which I'd been a riotous moron throughout the week. She then politely – contritely even – requested that I modified my behaviour in accordance with the guidelines that she helpfully set forth now. There were various mundane things, including doors that I hadn't been sufficiently neurotic about securing shut behind me, which in turn made my shower water a decibel more audible to her than it would otherwise have been, but the biggest extraction of urea was an immediate ban on morning kettle-use. Her bedroom was next to the kitchen and she was being woken up each morning by the sound of my obnoxiously boiling water to make coffee in an attempt to fortify my wits before setting off on my commute at 7 AM. A week later, she was leaving early and I was sleeping in. I woke up to what I thought was someone hammering a garden shed together outside followed by a monsoon hitting, but it was in fact the sound of my flatmate slamming doors and then taking a rambunctious shower. I'm pretty sure I also heard the kettle.

I was so terrified of poking the beehive of her indignation again that, a few days later, things got a bit silly. I had been out late and arrived home when she was already asleep. I was extremely hungry, having not eaten an evening meal. I had also not had chance to go shopping, meaning that the only food at my disposal now was a pasta microwave meal, purchased and frozen for a time like this. However, I had evidently forgotten at the point of sale that a time like this would involve using the microwave when my flatmate would be asleep. This would cause no less of a disturbance to her than if I had stampeded around the place in a deliberately elephantine manner, perhaps even playing the bagpipes all the while in an emboldened spirit of having nothing to lose. I was sufficiently housetrained to realise that I was banned from preparing food in the kitchen while she slept but I was not going to go to bed hungry.

The flat constituted the top floor of a three-storey house that was owned and occupied by a warm-hearted retired lady. Of course, my flatmate and I were both ultimately guests to the lady and theoretically equal to each other, despite the hierarchical dynamic that had evolved on the top floor. My flatmate sweetly conducted herself on the premises in a way that maximised courtesy to our host and I conducted myself in a way that neurotically endeavoured not to offend either of them. My flatmate and I lived almost exclusively in our self-contained upper quarters but descended to the ground floor to do our laundry, for which everyone in the house shared a room off the hallway. This room featured a toilet, sink, shower, washing machine and tumble dryer. It also contained, I gleefully now realised in the first moments of a plan that nocturnal hunger and a lack of third-party judgment occasioned me to miscalculate as genius, several electrical sockets. It was the perfect foil to the silence-in-the-kitchen policy. I would carry the microwave down two sweeping flights of uncarpeted stairs at half one in the morning, take it into a room that counted a lavatory amongst its amenities and heat my food in there. Nothing would say 'fuck the regime' with more gusto and I'd go to bed gastronomically satisfied.

I set off. The floor was nicely polished and the microwave was deceptively weighty. I really couldn't afford to do anything as farcical or cheaply predictable as dropping the appliance down the stairs. Moreover, I'd already made a name for myself in this house by setting off the burglar alarm within the first hour of my residency. For this reason, I had done a reccy before the microwave was transported down and had been in advance to switch the alarm off. A short time later, I made it to my destination with the microwave and set it down atop the tumble dryer, identifying this as the least eccentric cooking surface of those available. I then realised that the food was still upstairs so went back to retrieve it.

On my way back down, bashfully bearing a spinach and ricotta cannelloni, I noticed a camera installed in the hallway, pointing to the staircase. This would have been keeping a careful surveillance of my admittedly questionable culinary expedition. It constituted the third-party judgement that had not readily offered itself when I was conceiving the whole idea two floors heavenward. The landlady, who was a touch conservatively minded despite her many charms, would normally have been asleep on the first floor. However, she had gone away for a few days so I had casually ruled out the possibility of an awkward encounter. She was a French monarchist. I rather suspected that if she were still coming to terms with the relatively established concept of *La République*, the notion of her lodger microwaving a cannelloni in her downstairs lavatory in the early hours might have been an innovation too far.

I set the microwave going. By day, in the kitchen, the appliance seemed almost silent, but in a downstairs toilet in the middle of the night, it seemed to attain the decibel level of a ship's engine room. Ironically, I started to need the lavatory. I could not have predicted where the line of impropriety would be drawn in these circumstances but some clarity had now presented itself: it just wasn't cricket to take a leak in the room where one's evening meal was cooking.

I hoped now that these four minutes and thirty seconds of feeling increasingly self-conscious in front of my zero-strong audience would be worth it as I suddenly grew fearful of the inevitable beeps that would announce, with the pitch and volume of an ambulance's siren, the ready-to-eat status of my basic Italian repast. It now seemed that said beeps might be audible to the person residing two storeys aloft, for whose uninterrupted repose I was starring in this pantomime. My sense that I had overstepped the mark intensified further when the tomatoey aroma of the delicacy surreally started to fill the room. I hoped it would be gone by morning. I also hoped that the odour wouldn't adhere to my landlady's lacy smalls, which I now registered were hanging up in the corner. However, I quickly ceased to care about such, well, small matters, when it turned out that the landlady had come home earlier than planned and had been sitting in the adjoining room in her satin dressing gown throughout. Her head inquisitively introduced itself around the door.

Nothing prepares you for how much of a cockwomble you feel upon being discovered microwaving a cannelloni in a seventy-something French lady's downstairs toilet in the middle of the night. It was a new experience for us both. I embarked, in French of course and at a rather high octave, on a rambling explanation of how I was acting out of great courtesy to my flatmate at a time of exceptional personal hunger. I insisted that I was not intoxicated or dangerous but merely a bit simple. An increase in people of such immense thoughtfulness as me could, I just stopped short of venturing, make our planet a more harmonious place to live. I believed this to be the case even if neither my clones nor I would ever advance scientific discovery, much less qualify for a Nobel prize. The landlady's expression gradually changed from alarm to bemused charity. The situation clearly presented a challenge to her emotional literacy. 'Bon appetit,' she wished me in perplexed resignation before withdrawing. Maybe my people, with our lateral thought processes and our microwaves, are actually the undiscovered geniuses of the current age.

FIFTEEN

Temperature Regulation

The temperature is another major factor affecting how well you might sleep, and something on which an anxious host might be eager to hear a report the next morning. Many hosts get so movingly distressed about the possibility of your being too cold that they lay on a comprehensive selection of insulating accessories and heating appliances for your experimentation: blankets, hot-water bottles, electric heaters and so forth. People are often unsure as to how warm it might be in their spare bedrooms during the night, especially in the attic, so they might ensure that the heating is set to its maximum level of thrust. This often results in theirs being the only house in the street where the snow on the roof has melted, falsely advertising to neighbours and inquisitive police officers that illicit greenery is being farmed on the premises.

Warming Up the Room

I usually find that I'm warmer and cosier at night in other people's houses than I am in my own – at least if sleeping in a bedroom – because of this aforementioned care and attention on the part of hosts. As noted, they often leave the heating set at a higher temperature than one might at home because they'd rather endure a bigger bill than subject a guest to the novel malaise of waking up with icicles suspended from their nose. An extreme case of misguided decadence with heating appliances occurred when I stayed in a friend's living room in a draughty single-glazed Victorian apartment. I was sleeping on an airbed crammed in next to the fireplace and my friend had heartily, if not entirely sagely, encouraged me to turn on the electric fire – situated mere inches away from my face – if I felt cold during the night. Within minutes of getting into bed, I began to shiver. My less hardy extremities started to freeze over as if I were sleeping outdoors. Therefore, I took my friend up on her suggestion of using the fire and promptly dozed off in toasty contentment. I woke up a few hours later, convinced that I was on fire. A mirror reflected that my skin had adopted an arresting shade of burgundy. My eyes were painfully dry but the rest of me bathed in a deep lake of perspiration. Hastily, I deactivated the fire and let the room return to its previous sub-zero temperature. My heart rate eventually returned to normal and I fell back to sleep with the fulfilled serenity of a man who hasn't just died. At sunrise, I woke up shivering anew, this time to find a penguin at my bedside who jauntily tapped me on the shoulder with his flipper and asked what time he could expect breakfast to be served.

Of course, *hosting* guests can cause us to reflect on and learn about our own living conditions. I had the pleasure of hosting an acquaintance for the night some years ago, who created her ideal overnight temperature in my living room by turning the electric heaters up to full blast and then opening all the windows to their maximum extent. This was in a sixth-floor flat. The guest explained to me the next morning, with borderline piss-taking audacity, that that had been the only way of creating a climate that was anywhere near conducive to getting to sleep on my woefully uncomfortable sofa. It had been quite a windy night, as I gleaned when I then looked out of the window and registered that my vertical blinds were lying in a heap in the car park like struck-down kites, a hundred feet or so closer to the centre of the Earth than where I usually liked to keep them. My guest had also opened the balcony doors and I reflected during the painstaking hour it took to reattach the blinds that it would have been jolly unfortunate if she had sleepwalked and ended up joining them on the same pile.

Warming Up the Bed

There is a variety of ways in which a bed can be kept warm overnight. A friend of mine likes to give his a good wafting under the covers with the hairdryer for five minutes before he gets in, jumping aboard before the heat escapes. I suppose we have to get it where we can, but I'm not sure one can carry on like that in someone else's house in the middle of the night. A more likely creature comfort to be supplied by a host, particularly a host of a more traditional mindset, is a hot-water bottle.

What a curious invention the hot-water bottle is. Many of us make regular use of them and they transmit an immensely agreeable warmth to and through the body but there is something rather counter-intuitive about sharing one's bed with a vessel of scalding water. Of course, all hot-water bottles carry a warning telling you not to use boiling water, since damage to the rubber could lead to leaks, injury and general peril, but it is conceivable that a lot of hot-water bottles get taken to bed each night with their users having flouted this cautionary admonishment.

In an ideal world, kettles would have a hot-water bottle mode via which the heating procedure cut short before the water reached boiling point. That might be the best thing I've ever thought of, which is a rather downcast state of affairs after thirty-two years' occupation of the planet. It might also be the best idea that any big cheeses in the world of kettle manufacture have happened to read this week, so I invite any such people to get in touch and keep me in the loop regarding my cut of the billions that are to be made from the concept.

Of course, most of us regard it as only humane that the rubber water-receptacle is wrapped in a soft and snuggly cover to make it tactilely agreeable and indeed less likely to put you in hospital. Every so often, I come across someone who either doesn't realise that hot-water bottle covers are a thing or who sees them merely as a namby-pamby concession to having a nervous system. Indeed, some of my early experiences with hot-water bottles were like this. The bottle had to be carried to the bed at high speed like a sizzling skillet being carried to a table (in which context one would tend to wear oven gloves) and, once placed in the bed, one had to keep all indispensable limbs at a safe distance from it and generally fear it for at least thirty minutes until it had cooled down a bit. To have placed one's feet on the newly smouldering hot-water bottle would have been as reckless and punishing as sticking one's feet into a roaring fire. This was truly the naked light bulb of the bed-warming genre. One day, my grandmother showed me her splendid woollen hot-water bottle cover and I realised that not every hot-water bottle experience needed to involve adrenalin, trepidation or blistering.

Even more absurd than our modern practice of placing rubber containers of hot liquid in our beds is the bygone convention of using a ceramic equivalent, such as those to be found in museums, antique shops and perhaps in the bed of Jacob Rees-Mogg. How on earth did these work? Hot-water bottles regularly jump ship halfway through the night. What must have been the scene when one of these searing meteorites tumbled from the bed and crashed down onto the hard floor below? Did they break into pieces and release a torrent of hot water across the floor? Did the floor stop them at all or did they merely continue their gravid descent through the ceiling and into the living room below? Did everyone in the street wake up suspecting a bomb or an earthquake? I guess we should ask Jacob.

The main alternative to the hot-water bottle is the electric blanket. I have never owned such a thing. Just as it's a bit strange on the face of it to be climbing into bed with hot water, so too does it seem slightly dissonant to be lying on a plain of live electric heating elements. In the USA and Canada, it is apparently more common to sleep underneath the covering rather than on top of it. This strikes me as even more daring. I'd certainly think twice about lying on my back. A host might have left your electric blanket switched on in anticipation of your getting into bed. If they are especially attentive they might also mention that they have done this, thereby preventing you from waking up in the night resembling a piece of meat on a barbecue or with a flame-grilled whopper, as I believe they say in one of the global burger establishments.

At the time of writing, the relevant *Wikipedia* article solemnly notes that 'old or damaged blankets concern fire safety officials internationally'. Such items also reportedly account for around five thousand fires per year in the UK alone. How ironic that their ultimate *raison d'être* is to make us sleep more soundly. That said, electric blankets these days are relatively sophisticated, so a more recent example would hopefully disengage after a set period before a state of danger were to erupt. Moreover, the technology now enables the user to select which parts of the body are exposed to the most heat. Engaging in trial and error with these settings might see you greeting your host the next morning resembling a rasher of streaky bacon.

Cooling Down

There are various possibilities for warming yourself up, some more hazardous than others. But what if you need to cool down? This could be the case if your host has ended up over-catering for your thermal requirements and turning the sleeping environment into a sweltering inferno via a combination of leaving the heating on the highest possible setting and furnishing your bed with sturdy blankets or a thick duvet. Alternatively, you might be in an attic room that magnifies the ambient temperature outside, or it might just simply be a warm night. In the former case, things can probably be set back to normal by taming the radiator and peeling back the covers. However, if the room is too warm owing to reasons other than zealous human intervention, you will need to find an alternative solution that doesn't provoke any mayhem.

Perhaps the first course of action would be to continue peeling away layers of bedding, even until there is nothing left, and then consider how you might do likewise with your clothing. It must be stressed that the latter must be avoided if there is any chance of your dignity being compromised if, for instance, sleeping somewhere less than entirely private. After reducing your insulation in this way in order to get to sleep, you will probably wake up in the middle of the night feeling bitterly cold, prompting you to reinstate the blazing and highly insulated conditions with which you started and, in due course, waking up again in another torrent of sweat.

Another possible way of cooling down is via the opening of a window. If you are sleeping in an upstairs room, opening the window is both effective and reasonably foolproof. The exception is when staying in a room fitted with Velux windows. These are effective too – sometimes beyond one's imagining – but with the added novelty of allowing the rain to pour liberally into the room and flood the place while you are unconscious. If these windows are above the bed, this attribute can be useful because nothing cools you down at night like a cold shower from the heavens. Further side-effects of an open window are the potential insects, birds and even bats that might fancy popping in during the hours of darkness, respectively to dine on small portions of your skin or to attempt to redecorate the room with excrement.

If you are sleeping downstairs, opening the window carries more obvious risks. It is fine for ventilating the room before you go to sleep but, if you fail to close it before nodding off, you face the prospect of being woken up by a nocturnal balaclava-clad computer-repair person attempting to post themselves through the opening in order to take your host's laptop away for urgent maintenance. They will clumsily somersault down next to you and perhaps, assuming you are now awake, robustly request that you direct them to the item they have arrived to collect. Sadly, they might well show ingratitude and unreasonable irritation in return for your assistance and interest in their endeavours, their nerves frayed by the rigours of working so late and under such an acrobatically demanding regime.

Your room might be equipped with technological apparatus to assist in cooling you down, amongst which the most commonplace is the electric fan. I'm never quite sure if it's the done thing to leave one of these on all night, this perhaps being considered extravagant and thoughtless but, if you switch it off before going to sleep, you will likely return to your previous uncomfortable level of warmth before you have managed to nod off. If you leave a bedside fan on, you will, at some point either during the night or in the morning, wake up cold and with a stiff neck. The same dilemma exists with air conditioning, if you are staying somewhere that isn't the UK, only with the stiff neck swapped for the distraction of a loud hum. The sensation is created of sleeping next to a row of beehives in a monastery. Indeed, with this imagery in mind, one could almost be soothed to sleep amidst the buzzing. After all, one rarely encounters a sleep-deprived monk.

SIXTEEN

Animals: During the Night

Even if the family pets didn't interpret you at first sight as a self-propelled takeaway meal and start feasting on your extremities on your arrival, you might still encounter a labyrinth of animal-induced challenges after you think you've hidden away from the creatures-in-residence for the night.

While it is possible to animal-proof your belongings before you get into bed, it is rather more difficult to animal-proof your attempts to get to sleep. However over-indulgently the owner has attempted to communicate the evening's arrangements to their animal, stressing that your bedroom is out of bounds, the dog or cat typically doesn't take heed of the information. This is either owing to disbelief on their part that such a scandalous affront isn't a joke, or simply because dogs and cats don't have the powers of linguistic comprehension that might be imagined of them by someone whose bed is fitted with cat stairs.

Cats are particularly persistent and are likely to regard your occupation of their quarters as a matter of calculated injustice rather than as an innocent misunderstanding. They know that if they scratch loudly at the bedroom door for an hour or so as if attempting to excavate their way through, and punctuate the operation with indignant miaowing, you will yield and open the door to dissuade or remove them in your state of sleep-deprived frustration. However, as soon as the door is more than three inches ajar, the creatures will shoot into the room like police officers carrying out a raid.

'Split up!' the cat-in-charge might miaow to its colleagues upon entry. One cat will then commence circuits atop the bed to make you feel generally uneasy and dominated while another carries out a baggage inspection. Another will hurtle under the bed and smugly remain there, now untouchable.

Cat owners often tell you to 'just shoo them out,' should such feline invasion occur. How touchingly simplistic. Even if you manage to chuck out the first two in your state of weary rage, possibly after an hour of the animals taking it in turns to run back into the room when you open the door to evict the other, this third cat will wait out-of-reach under the bed until you fall asleep. Your next acquaintance will be when it climbs up to inspect your eyebrows at 4 AM. By this time, the cat's two comrades will have resumed their hysterical wailing and scratching on the landing. The whole thing is orchestrated to remind you that, if you had any decency, you'd take leave and go and sleep in the greenhouse. While we're on the subject, I believe it minimizes disharmony in the air the next morning if you remove the animals via the bedroom door rather than the adjacent window.

If you need to leave your room during the night in a house where cats operate, it is often not the animals themselves that will cause you a mischief. One of the most disagreeable night-time booby traps is the cat-litter tray, positioned to be discreet during the day and consequently invisible during the night. It is advisable to perform a visual risk assessment during waking hours so that your night-time movements in the communal areas don't take on an all-terrain element and cause you to experience the unwelcome and pungent underfoot sensation of gravel and mud, which will, in fact, be cat litter and the turds it attracts. If there are multiple litter trays about the house, it is probably wise to take an old pair of trainers to protect your feet from the odorous indignity of quite literally putting your foot in it. Of course, the trainers will need to be suitably softly soled to enable you to walk around at night with the furtiveness of the cat itself, although your exclamation when your foot makes contact with the waste product will probably awaken most of the street in any case.

Of course, not all pets are expected to be wandering around the house under sensible and predictable circumstances. It would be quite eccentric, for instance, to nip upstairs and meet a tropical fish sauntering down in the opposite direction. A lot of animal species typically live in their own enclosures within the house but things can still go wrong. I had a hamster who, when I went on holiday, was taught by my friends how to open his cage door – presumably in case of fire. This paved the way for eighteen months of his appearing in my bedroom in the middle of the night. If you think you have encountered a mouse during your stay, it is a good idea to delay your hysterical reaction for a few seconds until you're certain it isn't merely the family hamster heading out to the twenty-four-hour Tesco to top up his nuts.

If you happen to be sharing a room or even just a storey with a hamster, you will not be lonely because its nocturnal presence means that it'll be on hand like a miniature concierge to assist with any queries you may have during the night. It'll also run in its wheel all night with seemingly infinite energy, producing a sound similar in timbre and volume to that of a freight train. There's absolutely no chance of getting to sleep against this so you might as well put on a fitness DVD and join the hamster in its twilight exercise regime, building up a heart-warming if somewhat surreal sense of camaraderie with the animal. Your host will be delighted to learn over breakfast about your revelry with the rodent, not that you'll manage to wake up in time to recount the story before 4 PM. They might alternatively walk in and behold the scene for themselves before making a hasty retreat and vowing never again to eat cheese before bed.

Even if your sleep is undisturbed by the actions of the family pets, sometimes the mere knowledge that you are sharing a roof with certain creatures can be a barrier to contented repose. Some people voluntarily keep snakes in their houses and can quite contentedly go to sleep at night on the same premises. I wish the world's snakes well but am not terribly keen to make their acquaintance. I once stayed in a house where it was casually mentioned before bed that one of the pet corn snakes, wittily named 'Cornflakes,' had recently vacated its enclosure and hadn't yet been found. It had apparently disappeared under the recently varnished floorboards and could have resurfaced at any time. I spent my night in the living room in a state of wide-eyed unease. My buttocks attained the previously mentioned degree of clenching that could have enabled them to compete at international level, a state that became so entrenched that my trousers would barely hold up the next morning. The house was sold not long afterwards. The sales listing presumably didn't spoil the surprise that there was a scaly underground lodger who could come up for air and cause the new homeowner either an unrestrainable bowel movement or an instinctive departure through the nearest window.

The blood-thirsty dog that might have nibbled you on arrival might now be spending the night in a room comfortably separated and distanced from your own, after putting the fear of God (which is 'dog' backwards – surely no coincidence) into you when you first met. This offers the dog the privacy in which to plan your demise in peace. Of course, such segregation is also to give you a feeling of security against the animal, which may have been awaiting the unmonitored tranquillity of the early hours to tuck into you without the nuisance of other humans being on hand to intervene for your survival. However, the arrangement can break down, perhaps via a door negligently left unfastened by someone going to quench their twilight thirst.

I once stayed with a bouncer who removed a rather intimidating Dobermann to another room in the house before bed, all the while looking down at the creature sympathetically and saying 'Matthew doesn't like you'. This was all very well until the Dobermann and I coincided on the landing in the middle of the night. Our eyes locked through the tormenting sea of darkness. The beast fixed its gaze on me in an unapproachable manner, sensing my trepidation and basking in having the upper hand. He let out a mildly threatening grunt which I believe translated as 'You can keep your testicles this time'. I was relieved that we had at least been formally introduced before bed, despite our not exactly hitting it off, because I would otherwise presumably have been mistaken for a burglar and be penning this reminiscence with my one remaining finger.

SEVENTEEN

Stitched Up

Sometimes, even in an informal or relatively familiar environment where you don't think you need to be too precious about your conduct, you can still end up being left high and dry.

On a subsequent stay in the London apartment with the two bathroom doors, I assumed, however cockily, that I now had the place sussed. Following an evening of laddish banter and a glass of Robinson's Barley Water too many, I sauntered to the bathroom after lights-out in a nonchalant fashion. I was now wise to the facility's foible. Indeed, by this point, I had dined out on the previous experience occasioned by the facility's foible so many times that, in addition to my perceived certainty that there would be no repeat of the incident, this present bathroom trip bore a profundity beyond my mere bodily needs. It was a pilgrimage. My walk across the hallway would retrace the steps I took that fateful night. Once inside the bathroom, which I now realised had become a place of far deeper significance for me than it was for those who performed private routines in it each day, I would pause and marvel in solemn reflection upon the emotional white-knuckle ride that I endured the first time I stood on those cold floor-tiles. I would adopt the rueful smile that one sometimes wears when reflecting upon eccentric catastrophes.

My journey was easy. I now knew where to find the hall light switch and felt confident about using it, my hosts' bedroom door being sealed shut. Having concerned myself little with torches, tiptoeing or other hallmarks of rookie neuroticism, I arrived at the bathroom door and found it locked. I returned a little while later and it was *still* locked. The apartment was completely silent. As my need to pee gathered urgency, it became cripplingly transparent that my hosts had exited the bathroom via the private door into their bedroom, but had left the communal door bolted from the inside. Bollocks.

With my critical thinking now impaired by my condition, I desperately scanned the options. I initially considered whether there might be an alternative facility. The only accessible plumbed-in receptacle on the premises beyond the bathroom was the kitchen sink and, somehow, scrambling up onto the worktop and taking an aim didn't strike me as gentlemanly. Had I spontaneously been joined in the kitchen at any point by either member of the household seeking a badly timed glass of water, the sight of my pissing in the sink could have burned bridges. It might also have incited pangs of apprehension every time they found spilt apple juice on the worktop over the following days. No: even in a storm of this nature, this port was not an option. It did strike me that my ending up with company while spending a penny in the kitchen would have served me with the opportunity to request the unlocking of the bathroom door, but I was in no mood for irony.

What else could I have done? Navigating my way to the alternative bathroom entrance through the master bedroom via torchlight was an idea promptly dismissed for a variety of reasons, amongst the highest-ranking being that my bumbling presence could have been misinterpreted and I might have been received with a hearty thump. Filling an item of crockery with my urine struck me as being in a league of poor taste equivalent to relieving myself in the kitchen sink. There were no plastic bottles to hand and, in any case, I didn't fancy a situation where the substance would greet me when I woke up, to say nothing of my hosts' reactions on entering their living room early the next morning to find me in blissful slumber near a vessel of unpalatable fluid.

No solution being forthcoming within the apartment, I realised that I needed to think outside the premises. I considered petitioning social media to see if any London-based friends wouldn't mind allowing me to travel across from the Isle of Dogs in the middle of the night to use their WC. However, I decided against this. Ignoring the preposterousness of such a request, it seemed unlikely that anyone qualifying would still be awake to hear my plea.

I then considered public establishments. It was a Sunday evening, approaching midnight. There was a twenty-four-hour McDonalds a few miles away. This was looking like the only possibility. I would have to travel by taxi, being at a riverside location estranged from all other public transport at such a time. With my credulity feeling progressively stretched, I started to get dressed in order to put my plan into action.

It soon occurred to me that if I were to leave the apartment, I wouldn't be able to get back in again because the door would have locked behind me. No key had been left anywhere obvious because it had probably escaped everybody's scrutiny that I would require such a thing. This tied in with it also having slipped through the net that I might have wished to gain access to the lavatory. I could have propped the door open for the forty-five minutes or so that the operation might have taken but then I'd have been leaving my friend's entire home helplessly exposed to potential invasion by dishonourable individuals. Such people could have wandered in and helped themselves to the family silver, provided it wasn't stored in the bathroom. Even this plan – this completely rational and practical solution – had fallen at an early hurdle.

The only remaining possibility was to go home. I was going to have to flee the flat in London and leave a note to say that I had caught the train home to Leeds because I needed the toilet. Unfortunately, I'd also missed the last train. No matter, I could check into a hotel instead. That would effectively be the same thing as far as my hosts were concerned – I'd have escaped in the middle of the night and wouldn't be present to greet them cheerily or otherwise in the morning. At least all their mugs would be sterile, although it would pass by them that this constituted good fortune. Hopelessly, even less able to compute the absurdity of my plight than before, I made one final and pitifully desperate visit to the bathroom door and tried to open it. I let out a despondent weep – and fortunately nothing else – as the door remained steadfastly locked while the torrents raged in my bladder.

This time at the bathroom door, I noticed via some more focused observation that the lock was of the variety where one could undo it from the outside by inserting a coin. I could now see a potential light at the end of this tunnel of continence.

Thanking the Lord for his eventual provision of a way forward, I keenly went back to the living room to mine my pockets for currency. It probably wasn't entirely unpredictable, given the excruciating turn of events thus far, that I found them bare. I had been coasting contactlessly around the capital all day and hadn't envisaged needing to carry change in order to access my oldest friend's crapper. My predicament brought a new dimension to the need to 'spend a penny' although, had the bathroom door been contactless-enabled like the London Underground ticket barriers, I would gladly have coughed up the £2.40. I was almost back at square one when I caught sight of a jar of coins on a shelf.

I was going to need a small loan from this jar for the sake of my survival. By this point, I had no principles about raiding it and no fear of the consequences of being caught in the act. After all, it wasn't as if I would be making off with the coin after using it to open the bathroom door. My actions were perfectly innocent.

The shelf on which the jar was located was closer to the ceiling than to the floor. It had to be accessed either on tiptoes or by standing on a chair. I opted for the former, since that seemed the most efficient and noiseless option, and tentatively started unscrewing the jar's lid.

My advice at this point is that if you are ever in this situation, always stand on a chair. It will grant you an additional sixty or so centimetres' altitude, meaning that you won't need to tip the jar towards you to turn the lid. It will enable you to be looking down on the jar in confident control, rather than feebly stretching up to it. This in turn will eliminate the possibility of your hosts' money torrentially raining down on your face, as happened to me now. The coins raced each other to the hardwood floor, each one reporting its landing with a loud metallic thud and a celebratory roll underneath the sofa.

The shelf accommodating the coin jar was fixed to the wall that protected my hosts from an awareness of the trauma I was enduring on their premises. Thankfully, it wasn't the entire jar's worth of coins that spilled out but the jackpot-esque commotion could surely have awoken my friends. Perhaps this jar had been laid on as a test of my honesty, like with the sofa money in Chapter Ten. Maybe they knew I'd be tempted and had locked the bathroom door to stop me from going further and stealing the shaving foam. By any standards, I was not performing well. Even if I had managed to retrieve all the dispersed coins and put them back, the noise had done me no favours. I felt like I was in even deeper excrement when I registered that it was one of those digital jars that count the money. I would have bet my hosts would have known exactly how much was in there. Maybe they'd been saving up for a chamber pot for future guests and I'd been caught in the transition period between the bathroom being rendered out of bounds and such a repository being purchased.

I picked myself up, along with a penny from the floor. I was a fallen man but my acute bodily discomfort still reigned chief amongst my woes. I walked back to the bathroom door and inserted the currency into the lock.

I stopped in my tracks. Before turning the lock with the coin, I was suddenly paralysed by the 0.00000000003% chance that the room had in fact been occupied the whole time. Indeed, it potentially still was. Prizing open the door of an occupied bathroom could have suggested an unhealthy inquisitiveness on my part to the person receiving me on the other side. It would have made me appear no better than the man who forced entry to the WC in my workplace. It would certainly have been crossing a line. Everyone within earshot would doubtless have felt that the inevitably exchanged shrieks warranted further investigation.

I felt I needed a period of sustained vigilance just to be sure it was safe to proceed. I wasn't going to stand with my ear pressed to the door, thinking that not to be cricket, but I needed to know that my name wasn't mistakenly going to find itself on some official list of disreputable persons.

Another half-hour passed. The apartment remained silent. I suppose this owed largely to the prick sleeping in the living room having taken a break from dropping coins from a two-metre height.

Eventually, the moment arrived. Tensions running high and the banks of my personal river having almost burst, I cautiously unfastened the door. Various potential ironies were running through my mind. In the event of someone being inside, my guest appearance would see me on a conveyance back to Yorkshire after all, or at least on foot to a less comfortable sleeping place on the Isle of Dogs. Secondly, the hysteria would lead me to demonstrate involuntarily that the provision of a WC wasn't a strict requirement for enabling me to do what I needed to do. Gingerly, I allowed my head to lead the way and insert itself around the door ahead of my body. I squinted anxiously. This wasn't a time for high-definition imagery.

The room was, of course, empty. Obviously. My hosts had blissfully slumbered through my entire ordeal. They had been unconscious when I'd initially met with the consequences of their door-lock-related oversight and had remained so as I sat planning to head out into the night just to urinate. They had also, presumably, slept through the avalanche of copper. I could have climbed on a chair, lobbed the coin jar across the room while shouting 'tequila!' and then thrown myself to the floor, subsequently howling with the pain of two broken arms. They would not have stirred. The ecstatic release upon finally gaining entry to the bathroom caused me to repeat the clamorous and cartoonish routine of my previous visit and your expectations are unlikely to be subverted when I tell you that the door into my hosts' bedroom was wide open once again. Thankfully, for all I took leave of my gentleness when grabbing and slamming the door, I did at least do this *before* launching into the other ecstatic relief – the headline act – that was the ultimate objective of this bladder-wrenching operation. I'm not sure which genius drew up the internal layout of these apartments but I hope they've just drunk six litres of water and are now stuck in a lift.

Cause for Alarm

Further opportunities to be innocently framed when staying somewhere as a guest are offered by security systems. Alarms can present all sorts of peril. The most obvious example of this is when the alarm has not been mentioned and you open a door or cross a line that triggers it, usually at a distasteful hour. Sometimes, however, a host's tutorial on the alarm system can be so baffling that you breach the peace when trying to follow the instructions to switch it off or reset it. This is either through having misunderstood the intimidatingly complex guidance, or from your memory being clouded by fear of the consequences of error.

The most elaborate domestic security situation I ever encountered was in the house that played host to the night-time microwave episode. The proprietor, who was as perturbed by the possibility of intruders as she was by the reality of French republicanism, kept the burglar alarm on at all times of the day and night, even when we were all in the house. Most of my first hour on the premises was taken up with a lengthy demonstration of the alarm system's modus operandi. The system had to be deactivated each time one went downstairs and then reactivated before either returning upstairs or leaving the house.

A pitifully short time after my induction, I descended the stairs from my room on the second floor and, when I arrived at ground level, the alarm duly started to bleep its fifteen-second countdown to detonation. My host had thoughtfully written down the code for me on a piece of paper, which I had then placed on the bedside table two storeys above. It impractically now remained where I had put it. There was little chance of me making it there and back in fifteen seconds. I didn't even try. I froze helplessly as the alarm promptly howled and shrieked as if I were standing in a jeweller's shop while wearing a balaclava and waving a pistol. My host quickly arrived at the top of the stairs with her ear to the phone, reassuring the person on the other end that she was at home and all was well. It transpired to be a monitored alarm. Had the lady not been at home, she informed me in a manner of sufficient gravity as to focus my mind for the rest of my stay, the police would have turned up. I imagined that I would be seeing a lot of them as the days unfolded.

A much more primitive burglar-deterrent was my friend's system of wind chimes that hung a short distance above the bannister in his cottage. 'This is my burglar alarm,' he proudly told me on my first visit, gesturing at the installation of clanging and tinkling. 'It's impossible to go up the stairs without knocking it all.' He was quite right. I stayed at his house once and arrived back quite late, whereupon I stumbled into the wind chimes as per his design and provoked a jangling of new-age serenity which, contrary to the pacifistic intentions of the chimes' creators, provoked my friend to appear from his bedroom door in the slightly paradoxical state of wearing a blue stripy night cap and wielding a baseball bat. Wind chimes have often been believed to ward off evil. Seemingly, one way in which they do this is to summon a defensive householder to clobber evil in the unmentionables and pin it to the ground until the police arrive.

There is a story about two priests walking, for reasons unknown, through the woods in a state of complete nudity. A parishioner happens upon them, causing them to take evasive action. The first one covers his private parts and runs. The second one covers his face and does likewise. 'I don't know about you,' says the second one to the first, 'but in my parish, it's my face they recognise.' These men of God were at least able to cling to a small chance of anonymity between them. A similar fate to that of these hapless clerics can befall those who stay with people who, in the interests of security and vigilance, set you up to serve them with visual spectacles via the planting of closed-circuit television cameras.

My first experience of this was during a stay in an Airbnb, in which I occupied the spare bedroom of an apartment lived in by a young couple and an elderly aunt. The bedroom and communal bathroom were only a couple of metres apart across the hall, which was small, white and windowless. It also offered a bewildering choice of six also-white and closed doors from which to choose upon exiting the bathroom. This micro-hallway was fitted with security cameras that directly faced the room in which I was sleeping, presumably to dissuade guests from straying into the kitchen, breaking the chairs and eating the porridge. This setup guaranteed to supply its owners with televisual footage of their guests' every trip to and from the bathroom, despite having sought no filming consent from the cast or offered a performing rights fee. From the moment I arrived, I was, partly thanks to sleep deprivation, producing short silent movies in which I pathetically attempted to pick out the bathroom light switch from a choice of five possibilities located on the same panel in the hallway, plunging myself into darkness at least twice during each round of endeavour. This routine would be followed by my emerging from the bathroom and then freezing on the spot for a moment's prudent consideration before being sure I had selected the correct door to regain access to my bedroom. I must have presented as somewhat simple to those tuning in.

As the stay unfolded, my cinematic contributions developed beyond the increasingly predictable 'man selects light switch' motif. My modesty having come close to starring in a London stage-spectacular relatively recently thanks to the incident with the two-door bathroom, I was wise enough to take steps to avoid a risqué small-screen debut in this second apartment. I was careful not to do anything so banal or slapstick as take a chance on nakedly running back to the bedroom from the bathroom and realise too late that I was being broadcast into my hosts' kitchen. Their breakfast appetites would have dissipated at once. My attention to detail, however, sadly did not extend to ensuring that the door was properly secured once I had arrived back inside my bedroom after my shower.

In the narrow time window between removing my towel and donning my clothes, the door gradually fell open and my disrobed anatomy emerged with artistic gradation into the camera's line of vision. I was the rabbit caught in the proverbial headlights, defenceless and quite literally exposed. I dived at once to the floor behind the bed as if taking cover from a shower of bullets. This must only have added to my inadvertent self-portrayal as a clodhopping twat. What was my next move? My clothes were on the other side of the room and any attempt to retrieve them would have reinstated me to the broadcast, except this time on a rather undignified all-fours.

Realising that Plan A, which was simply to stay down there for the rest of my life, could have led to a yet more compromising situation if my hosts had come to investigate after a few days, I decided to pull the white duvet cover down to the floor. Moments later, the camera would record a mummified figure rising from the trench, hopping to the door and closing it. I was so impressed with my initiative and survival instinct that I considered asking for a copy of the footage. With hindsight, of course, it would have mattered little if I'd flaunted my wares and strutted to the door like a peacock because everything I had to offer had already been viewed. Since I was leaving at 5 AM on the morning of departure to catch an early flight, long before my hosts were awake, the technology meant that I was able to take a bow, smile to the camera and mouth my appreciation for a lovely stay as I let myself out.

EIGHTEEN

Objects

It is not just humans and animals with which a house guest potentially co-exists. In every house lives a motley variety of objects, some more inanimate than others, variously 'beautiful or useful' (to paraphrase William Morris) to their owners but of potential bemusement or peril to visitors. The props to be found lying around someone's house can tell us a lot about the person. For instance, a host's undisclosed bagpipe-playing habit could be exposed by the tell-tale presence of a chanter or a stack of neighbourly complaint letters. Alternatively or additionally, objects in a person's home can affect our sleeping experience on their premises.

Ticking clocks are largely inaudible against the other noises of daytime. However, as soon as you switch off the light and put your head on the pillow, they sound as if you have activated a time bomb. The clock's mildly ominous countdown begins to punctuate the silence with the timbre and tempo of a geriatric woodpecker, meticulously keeping tally of every second of missed sleep but also teasingly suggesting an impending explosion or similarly catastrophic disturbance. What is more, some clocks, in a perfectly dysfunctional marriage between the worst of the old and new, feature a ticking sound that has been installed in the device owing to the clock mechanism itself producing no natural sound. That's rather like shaving your head as a disguise and then wearing a hat. It is very silly indeed.

My grandparents were the proud owners of two very fine old clocks, one of which hung in the hallway and another that sat atop the mantelpiece in the lounge. The former had a pendulum and a weighty ticking sound and chimed to celebrate each quarter-hour. The latter produced a more agitated-sounding double-tick for every second and was usually out of sync with its colleague in the hallway. This created an unsettling soundtrack that implied that the end of the world would be later that afternoon and therefore the ironing desperately needed to be finished as soon as possible. While they occasionally overlapped, the mantelpiece clock usually chimed when the other one wasn't chiming, meaning that there was perpetually a fiesta of clanging taking place. On the hour, which was rarely the exact same moment in both rooms, the clocks would both erupt into a jubilant cacophony of Westminster Quarters that rendered all attempts at conversation futile until the renditions were complete. It must be said that it was all rather charming and the Westminster Chimes will always evoke happy memories of my grandparents' house. That said, those staying the night on the premises didn't always find that the musical timekeeping served as a soothing lullaby.

My aunt once stopped both these clocks at about 3 AM, after several sleepless hours' worth of recitals, just as one might equally remove the battery from a more modern clock to discontinue the ticking. If you stop a clock during the night, as she discovered, you will inevitably forget to set it going again the next morning. This will create a whirlwind of temporal disorientation in which one person goes to work early, one person goes to work late and one person goes back to bed under the impression that it is still only 3 AM.

A lot of clock devotees conversely find the silence as disturbing as other people might find the chiming obtrusive. Having been long accustomed to the constant company of one, my grandparents might have found a ticking clock's sudden absence to be highly unnerving. Without the reliable affirmation of the seconds passing, it may have felt for them as though time itself had stopped. Still, if you happen to be an enthusiast of chiming clocks and find yourself sleeping in the home of somebody who does not own one, it is probably a good idea not to bring anything along that will chime the hours. Your plans for the next morning could be thrown into disarray if you end up having to have your timepiece surgically removed.

It is probably not sensible to tamper with clocks in communal areas unless they're in the room in which you happen to be sleeping. Even in bedrooms, one has to be careful. An Airbnb host in London once caught me temporarily removing the battery from a ticking bedroom clock in order to get a good night's sleep and assumed I was in the business of stealing it. He assured me that there would be an inventory taken of all batteries and light bulbs before my departure and that I would be paying for any that were missing. I think he'd marked my card as soon as he knew that I was from somewhere north of Hertfordshire.

You might encounter your host's clothes in unexpected ways. Many years ago, I slept on a sofa near a clothes horse on which my host had immodestly opted to hang an assortment of her drying lingerie. After night had fallen, the room was comprehensively sealed from all sources of natural light. The clothes horse was on my flight path to the door. All was well until I attempted to find my way out of the room through the darkness in order to use the bathroom. Almost as if by design, I piled comprehensively into the exhibition of undergarments, which reliably collapsed to the floor and shed its merchandise with an ungraceful and dispassionate efficiency. It struck me that this was the closest thing I'd ever had to a one-night stand. There was an argument for painstakingly rehanging the garments in the order in which they had been before my collision, so as not to project the impression that I'd whiled away the night trying them on or browsing them to feel the softness of the material. However, there was an even greater argument for not spending any time at all with the undergarments and just leaving my clumsy demolition work to speak for itself. This I did, and it subsequently did not occur to me to mention my brief encounter with the underwear the next morning.

To my considerable regret, the clothes horse's fall had been broken by my open suitcase, which later transpired to have collected some of the smalls. I hastily later threw my things in my case the next morning and thought nothing more of the incident until I got home and unpacked in front of the then lady of the house, whereupon a black brazier emerged that had discreetly camouflaged itself against the black shirt and black trousers in my black suitcase and smuggled itself over the border into Yorkshire as a stowaway. I almost found myself wishing I'd had an actual one-night stand as it would have been easier and quicker to explain. I dare say there might also have been a more favourable ratio of pleasure to retribution. The other side of this bind, which was nothing more or less than a freak incident, was that I had effectively stolen my friend's bra. Attempts to explain the situation to the lady at home did not paint me in a good light as a convincing raconteur, a quick thinker or a credible human being. Meanwhile, I was left cold by a brief contemplation of how I might explain to the lady who hosted me, if pressed, the reason for her now having one bra fewer than the previous day. For all either of the females in this sorry triangle could have read the situation, my part in the migration of this foundation garment was rather less innocent than a mere clothes-horse collision. The garment's owner and I haven't spoken since. Neither the victim nor the perpetrator of a bra-related crime really knows who should make the first move afterwards, or indeed what that move should be.

One household accessory that can be relied upon to keep you awake at night is taxidermy. I was once left alone in an apartment where a former weasel posed on a shelf as if ready to pounce. I never fully trusted it not to be merely sleeping, waiting for me to turn my back or doze off and make myself vulnerable to a savage attack. Maybe that's what actually happens at Madame Tussauds. Perhaps Britney Spears and the Prince of Wales breathe sighs of relief at the end of each day and roam around the place to their hearts' content after closing time, perhaps kicking back with a pizza, before recommencing their tedious routine of pretending to be waxy and inanimate for the visitors' photographs the next day.

Even if the taxidermied creature has been deprived of its legs and body, and presumably therefore its ability to stroll over and maim you or chase you up the stairs, there is something slightly off-putting about being watched. I remember being told by a Parisian host family that I could use the piano in their opulent drawing room. I tentatively went downstairs and switched on the light in said room and was instantly received by the menacing glare of at least forty pairs of eyes and their associated open jaws and sharp teeth. My bowels nearly had a crisis of composure. I didn't hang around.

While guests do not appreciate spectators – stuffed or otherwise – at moments that are best kept private, it would seem that many hosts are happy to have an audience for their personal particulars. People are often extremely transparent with and unembarrassed by the sensitive and confidential items that they leave lying around. One sometimes learns, quite often against one's will, the finer details of one's host's medicaments, bedroom affairs, financial situation and impending court proceedings via the items casually strewn around in one's path when innocently attempting to use the room as offered as a place of repose. For my part, I cannot make it too plain that I do not go in search of these things. I have no remote wish to know about the contraceptive measures taken by members of the household or how many times more than me they earn, but how on earth am I prevented from inheriting this information if the relevant and bold-lettered documentation is unfolded across the nightstand like a bedtime story?

Sometimes, it is not so much the objects themselves that are unusual but simply where they are kept. I am always mildly amused by my friend keeping a sizeable library of DVDs in the downstairs toilet. It must be an outstandingly grave case of the shits where one has time to watch an entire film as the ordeal unfolds. More perplexing than this is the hygiene minefield that is the selection of throne-side books or magazines that are sometimes found adjacent to the porcelain in the homes of those who must appear to be exercising their intellect at all times. Not even when they're taking a dump can it seem that they are having a break from being academic or cultured. These editions are often artistically positioned, like coffee-table books. There is a strong implication that you might like to avail yourself of them but one is acutely aware that these pages have been turned by hands that were not in their most pure state. Of course, you will be washing your hands on the completion of business whether or not you've spent your time reading about the Bauhaus but there is still something unsettlingly contaminating about the whole thing. One also wonders if the volumes making up these lavatorial libraries are periodically returned to shelves elsewhere in the house to be exchanged for other titles. People borrowing them from the living room would be completely ignorant of their unsterile adventures. It is probably best not to think about it.

Of almost equal eccentricity is the provision of books intended to be read in the bath. Just how on earth do people manage this? It's like a less edgy version of reading a book while standing over a roaring fire. For the book not to be ruined, one would surely have to adopt a bodily position so rigid and precise that the bathing experience would resemble a sort of aquatic yoga session. Moreover, one would surely have to lower oneself into the bath without wetting one's hands. Even if this is successfully executed, and no doubt many people can and *do* do this with perfect poise and elegance, one wrong move would see the book submerged into the lathery abyss. It would later emerge resembling a chunk of toilet paper, a substance chosen for its purpose on account of the same absorbent characteristic that makes a book and a bath so incompatible. It's all a bit much for me.

Some people have items that would not be eccentric if they only had room for them. I knew a professor of music who spent several years living in one room but still with a concert grand piano, under which he was forced to sleep. It must have been a brave and adventurous lady who risked both the idiosyncrasy and the potential for concussion in the event of a night of passion, although the man's attempts to seduce potential candidates with salacious pianistic wordplay helped to ensure that the suitability of the bonking quarters remained a matter as academic as he was.

Similarly, I once slept in a small room that contained a lot of harps. I was on a sofa bed and enclosed on three sides by a delicate fortress of celestial instruments that cast eerie shadows against the wall. There was perhaps nothing surprising about the avant-garde improvisation I unintentionally performed on one of the instruments at 6 AM when I got up and tripped over one of the instrument's pedals. More arresting still was the scene as my misstep provoked three harps to tumble over in the most terrifying and potentially costly domino effect I have ever experienced.

In addition to objects around which you might have to tread carefully, there will usually be an assortment of items that have been laid on for your comfort and pleasure. A kindly and doting host might have left you something edible and tasty, for instance. Whatever has been left out for you, it is important to use it correctly in addition to showing immense gratitude for it. A hotel on the Isle of Skye received a review a little while back that was laudatory of everything apart from the 'gritty' bar of soap, which 'left an oily residue in the shower'. The guests, it transpired, had been attempting to wash themselves with a complimentary bar of tablet, the sugary Scottish confection. If one were to bring an error of this nature to light when staying with a friend, the host would likely dine out on the story until the day they died.

My aunt recounts a tale of her friend being presented with some clothes to put on at some point during a hospital stay. There was a gown, some socks and, bizarrely she thought, a cap. The nurse returned some moments later to find the lady sitting on the bed, having dutifully donned the apparel. 'That's not a cap, love, it's a pair of knickers,' the nurse explained with professional restraint. I'm not sure why I recount this tale because it's unlikely that your host will be providing you with underpants or indeed that there could be a second person this side of the Moon who might accidentally crown their head with a pair of undercrackers in sober circumstances. As with all the issues tackled on these pages, however, forewarned is forearmed.

NINETEEN

Waking Up

It is assumed, whatever mishaps may have occurred during the hours of darkness – and you may of course have spent an entirely peril-free night and consequently now written this book off as the planet's most absurd work of hyper-neuroticism – that you eventually went to sleep. It is also therefore assumed, unless something has gone monumentally and terminally pear-shaped, that you will at some point wake up.

Waking up in a strange house – and by a 'strange house' I merely mean a house other than one's own – is a peculiar business. I usually find that the first few seconds of consciousness serve as a mildly surprised reminder of where I went to sleep the night before, my internal hard drive having partially wiped clean overnight. Unless you've forgotten to close the curtains and been awoken by a tediously early sunrise, much of what unfolds in the first hour of waking depends on how you and your host left things the previous evening.

One thing about which I always forget to inquire until it's too late is the household's approximate getting-up time. Asking about this before bed is a good habit to get into. If there has been some discourse about the getting-up time and the general agenda for the morning, you should be okay to set your alarm for a civilised hour and not worry about being in the wrong place, i.e. bed, at the wrong time. If you have gone to bed uninformed, however, you must set your alarm for approximately 5 AM and spend at least three hours thereafter in a sleep-deprived yet hyper-vigilant state, listening out for signs of life. If you do this, it is unlikely that anybody will get up before 9 AM but, if you do not align your time of waking with that of the dawn chorus, you will almost certainly be awoken by your host knocking on the door and asking, in a pointedly urgent tone, whether you are up yet. You and your host might be going somewhere together and it might be heavily implied that you are the proverbial albatross around the neck of the morning's punctuality. Of course, your host could alternatively be knocking on your door at sunrise because they need to borrow another pair of handcuffs from the wardrobe. If this is the case, you'll have chance to sleep for at least another hour – provided the walls are sonically opaque – and be very glad indeed to be comatose while the criminal is being punished.

So, let's say you have woken yourself up early for no good reason and are therefore exhausted. You initially strain your senses to gauge whether or not your reluctantly prompt self-vivification has been in vain. Can you hear anyone moving? Can you tell where they are or what they might be doing, within the realms of good taste? Can you somehow hear if they might be dressed and poised to start the day? Do you hear running water from the bathroom or talking in the kitchen? Can you smell coffee or toast or bacon? As soon as you start to detect these various signs of life, perhaps it is time to bestir and present yourself. On the other hand, you may detect none of these things and sod's much-maligned law dictates that this will be the day that no one's getting up until lunchtime and everyone else has been made aware. If it does indeed transpire that you are awake redundantly early while being unsure of the time at which you are expected to rise, you now can't go back to sleep lest you doze beyond the point at which you should be up. The only way in which any of this neatly works out for the better – and this is itself bittersweet – is that such a conundrum becomes so maddening and exhausting that you eventually need to lie down, which happens to be just what you're presently doing. Your eager alarm, meanwhile, could have temporarily awoken other people. They will not remain conscious for long, but they will mutter drowsily about what a prick you are before going back to sleep for another five hours while you lie there in a wide-eyed state of anxious uncertainty.

'Just get up when you want in the morning,' an emptily reassuring line thrown in by hosts to establish cheerful informality, really means no such thing. It is, of course, a device for making a guest feel at home, presenting the morning regime as relaxed and approachable. That said, in practice, you don't want to be sleeping past a time that makes you look ungraciously out of sync with the rest of the household, hence the potential situation described in the previous paragraph, and this is especially the case if sleeping in a communal area. If you're sleeping on the sofa of a one-bedroom apartment where the kitchen and lounge are combined and your hosts need to have breakfast before going to work at 8 AM, it will enhance your credibility if you're not unconsciously sprawled out as a snoring speedbump while they consume their muesli. There is also the matter of FOMO (Fear of Missing Out).

What if your host prepares a lavish banquet of a breakfast and you miss it because you were just getting up when you wanted? I have sometimes sent text messages to hosts when it has got to around 9:30 AM and the house still seems to be silent. Has everyone gone out for the day and forgotten I'm there? Has everyone gone out for the day *because* I'm there?

You might wake up to the sound of distant voices, making you feel like you've missed out on all sorts of things already. The voices are a sign that people are up and conversing fluently. The sound of ceramic contact from the kitchen might suggest that householders are eating together while you're lying there idly and missing out on banter and breakfast. Alternatively, the sound of voices on waking can make one want to roll over and go back to sleep. I once stayed with a couple who heatedly whiled away the evening in full-throated disagreement on various matters, chief of which seemed to be the notion that the man was an irredeemable bastard with dire shortages of industriousness and understanding. I woke up the next morning to an impassioned decibel level that confirmed the ongoing opposition of the two points of view.

Some households have their own more distinctive ways of starting the day. I once stayed with some friends who told me the night before that they always drank tea in the morning. They then asked if I'd like some and, if so, what my preferences were regarding milk and sugar. I thought this was adorably thoughtful although it seemed a somewhat extravagant spectacle of organisation to be discussing such particulars the night before the tea would be consumed. Could I not have simply poured my milk in when we were downstairs drinking the tea as the day began? However, I had misunderstood the routine. At sunrise, as I was waking up, there was a gentle tap on my bedroom door. My friend then serenely appeared in the room in her night apparel with a cup of tea for me, made to my precise requirements as specified before bed. It was a delightful gesture that made my heart feel as warm as the tea.

The opportunity for a more abrupt awakening is offered by the host who cooks bacon in the morning, ensuring five-star reviews from omnivorous guests but habitually setting off smoke alarms in the process. The triggered alarm acts as a signal to the chef that the bacon is ready and to the rest of the household that bacon is available. The loud bleeping will typically be complemented by a lot of shouting from the cook, the slamming of at least one door and some blunt and off-target stabbing of the ceiling in attempts to silence the device. It is advisable to wait a few minutes for your host's blood pressure to return to normal before presenting yourself on the scene, however much of a hint this hullabaloo might have been that it was time you were up, because the person slaving over the grill or frying pan might not be in a mood where guests and kitchen implements are a healthy combination.

Households with children sometimes offer a dose of juvenile naïvety to kick-start your day. During an overnight stay before the current era of everybody having fifteen digital devices each from the age of four, my friend's host's nine-year-old son bounded into the guest room at 6:30 AM, turned on the family computer and proceeded to play the then-popular *RollerCoaster Tycoon 2* game. The early-rising infant learned some lusty new words as my friend was torn from slumber by the screams of the virtual masochists aboard the Inverted Hairpin Coaster hurtling around an improbable bend.

In vivid contrast with the wide-eyed innocence of a child wanting to create fairground rides, your day might begin with a remorseless invasion in the form of an undiscussed tradesperson visiting to do something drastic and inconvenient in the vicinity of your bed. This is more likely to happen if you are staying with somebody in a rented property where the landlord might have dispatched someone to do some work early in the morning and not kept your host fully in the loop. The labourer in question will be someone in possession of both their own key to the property and a firm belief that the action of knocking on a door serves as a warning of impending entry rather than as a polite request for it. The vocal tones announcing the tradeperson's arrival will be as indelicate as the words they convey. Some of these words might serve to ensure you understand that the working day of the lady or gentleman speaking them started at 6 AM, something that will be worn as a badge of honour in the presence of workshy layabouts who are still asleep two hours later. Your rest will terminate, in however abrupt or undignified a manner, when Mr or Mrs Fix-It dictates.

I once stayed overnight with a friend after having been out celebrating his birthday until the early hours. At a time that could not have been beyond 8:30 AM, I blearily got up and left the room to open my floodgates and subsequently arrived back at the doorway to behold the unexpected reality of a brusque and wild-haired man prizing up my bedroom's floorboards. He had made such rapid progress with this during what I had thought had only been a ten-minute absence on my part that there was now an insurmountable hole between the door and my bed. Indeed, I wondered how the man was going to make it back to civilisation himself. I immediately assumed that at least one of my drinks the previous evening had been spiked and that I was hallucinating.

'Oh, were you sleeping in here?' he asked at length. 'I wondered who this suitcase belonged to.'

I congratulated him on his aptitude for joining the dots, especially at so early an hour, and he made it clear that I would not be doing any further sleeping in there until the following nightfall. Of course, he'd been up since 5 AM and, in the three-and-a-half intervening hours, had been for a jog, built a house and milked a goat. I'd just been comatose during that time and probably wouldn't contribute anything useful to society even when I managed to dress myself and start the day, his demeanour implied. As I now sat evicted on the sofa downstairs and reflected on the experience, it struck me that the man could have appeared in a balaclava and requested my assistance with carrying the television out to his van to be taken away and cleaned, or even treated for woodworm. For all I'd been briefed that anyone was expected, combined with it not being the time of day to find me at my most mentally astute, I'd probably have obliged. Guests do not typically make the best security guards as they naïvely assume that everything unfolding around them is above board and that everyone else present surely knows more about the operations of the household than they do.

Houses attracting a particularly indiscreet breed of tradesperson are those occupied by students. I once met an electrician who was frequently contracted to do jobs in such properties, many of which necessitated moving furniture. 'If you go in in the morning,' he disclosed as if this were advice on which I might someday rely, 'it's usually easier just to move the bed with the student still in it.' 'The student' was portrayed as a moribund and nameless species, ranking somewhere on the hierarchy between domestic animals and people. I can think of little that would make my bowels give way with more immediacy than waking up to an anonymous bearded man taking hold of my bed and moving it with rogue insensitivity. I meant to ask the electrician if he wore a groin guard when going about his business in this manner.

The same gentleman effected a compromising incident a short time later when a student landlord had failed to disclose that a cupboard formerly housing the fuse boxes had been converted into a shower room. Entirely predictably, the elephantine electrician unwittingly entered the new facility while a hapless young woman stood bare within, occasioning such a shrill duet of distressed vocalisations that the entire storey required reglazing. If you're staying the night in a student house, it's probably best to take advantage of all available locks and then set your alarm for 5 AM so that you're awake at the same time as anyone who might be planning to call in with a licence to drill.

There is a chance of being awoken by someone else's alarm. A person's choice of alarm tone often serves as an extension of their personality and paints the guest a yet more vivid picture of the true character of their host. A traditionally minded host might still charmingly be using an alarm clock with a monotonous bleep or perhaps a crackly radio. Someone trying to be a hipster or who likes uploading photos of their home decor to Instagram might have an artificially antiquated analogue item. This will have a loud and persistent tick like a dozy woodpecker, while its alarm will be of such clamour that a typical day will start with a minor heart attack.

If your host is using the alarm on their phone, which is probably more likely in this day and age, you could be awoken by anything. It could be your host's favourite song or the theme music to their most loved television programme. It could be the classic iPhone *Radar* number, which summons me to life each morning while inducing a certain resentment for the new day. The most abruptly I have ever shat myself awake during adulthood was during a recent stay with a friend who was sleeping in the next room with the door open. At 7 AM, in a menacing tone and through the darkness, pulsated: 'EAT, eat, eat, eat, eat, eat, eat, eat... FLESH, flesh, flesh, flesh, flesh, flesh, flesh, flesh... lamb, chicken, beef, human, what's the difference?' My host said that this was the most effective alarm he'd ever used to terminate slumber. I found that thoroughly believable, although I dread to think how many new bed sheets he must have had to buy during the acclimatisation period with his cannibalistic companion.

TWENTY

Animals: The Next Morning

Even if you've made it through the night without disturbance or injury from another species, you might still wake up to find that you have company. While certain possible explanations for this are beyond the scope of this book and none of my business, it could be the case that your sleep is terminated by something furry climbing into your bed or licking your face, often having had the hours of darkness to chew its way out of its own nocturnal confinement and into yours.

Cats and dogs – cats especially – tend to have a slightly different body clock from humans or, at least, a different body clock from me. When I have stayed with dog owners, their faithful companions have usually heralded the new day with fanfares of barking, followed by a tour of the bedrooms to make sure no one has overslept.

Cats, if they ever left you alone in the night, will invariably find a way of gaining access to your bedroom at sunrise. They will then proceed to march in, disregard your personal space and inform you that your period of rest is up. They want feeding. They want an end to your trespassing. They make it clear that, if you are to remain on site, it must be to serve them. You can attempt to ignore them but this will be interpreted as a lack of comprehension that can only be addressed by intensifying their campaign of head-butting. They might even try incentivising you to bow down to their wishes by presenting you with whatever prized game they have bravely hunted and slain on their nocturnal neighbourhood prowl. The gift of a freshly caught dead bird on your pillow at dawn is a level of emotional blackmail to which freely distributed packs of charity Christmas cards can only aspire.

I have often stayed with a friend whose cat silently comes into my room at the crack of dawn, followed shortly by my friend charging in behind it shouting 'TILLY, NO! LET HIM SLEEP!' with no apparent concept of irony. This usually takes place too early for me to be able to converse with much eloquence or charm and so I pretend to be asleep until the hapless duo has vacated. Of the two of them, it is difficult to regard the cat as the problem.

It may be that you and an animal end up forming a hapless double act that makes it its business to wake up the entire household. Equally, the animal might use you as a gullible accessory with which to summon its owners. I once slept a Friday night on a friend's sofa and was joined at daybreak by an energetic Jack Russell terrier who expertly opened the living room door and started pacing the room before jumping up at the patio doors in an expectant manner. The dog clearly wished me to open the door so that it could go outside and secrete some turds in the garden, into which guests at the afternoon's barbeque could merrily step. The dog jumped on me and stared me hard in the eye. I inferred that any failure on my part to comply with the dog's wishes would result in it relieving itself into my shoe, which it had already measured up as a backup plan before petitioning me.

Sleepily, for it was a mere 6 AM, I rose from my pit as the dog continued to leap up against the glass portal to the outside world. I released the catch and opened the patio door, immediately triggering a piercing siren that reverberated through the house and possibly the postal area as if I'd swiped a loot of diamond rings from a jewellery shop or unwittingly opened – not for the first time in my life – an emergency door in Sainsbury's. My heart attained a level of pulsation that would have been more gratifying had there not been a dog involved. Then, in the manner of a firefighter responding to an emergency call, my friend promptly shot down the stairs eight-at-a-time like a sack of parsnips attempting a gymnastics routine, all the while dressed not unlike Fred Flintstone and having apparently profited from the services of the same barber. He bluntly silenced the pandemonium with a four-digit code.

'Alarm was on,' he explained redundantly and with a marked lack of poetry.

It then sprang to my mind, embarrassingly, that this early morning roll call had been entirely avoidable because I had stood and watched my friend set the alarm before we went to bed. Indeed, we had spoken of how nice it would be to have a leisurely Saturday lie-in.

'Sorry – I didn't think you'd be up!' I offered in a misjudged attempt at levity. It cut no mustard. There was a non-verbal mutual understanding that I was a twat but that all would be well if we both slept for another few hours and didn't prolong the present rendezvous. The dog didn't give a shit about the disturbance caused, presumably because any shits it may have carried in reserve had just been given to the long grass outside. The animal had exploited my naïvety and my slothful dawn brain power. It was ironic that all this had been in the name of avoiding indoor canine defecation because the alarm's frightful decibels almost prompted the humans to issue an involuntary bowel movement themselves.

Once the family pets have established their dominance over you by deciding how much sleep you're allowed, they might then refuse to let you enter the bathroom unsupervised. A cat in particular might stage a protest in the form of standing in the bathroom doorway to prevent you from securing yourself inside. In a spirit of compromise, it might allow you to pass but will then keep an eye on you while you self-consciously attempt to pass something else, rather like a prison officer accompanying an inmate to make their ablutions. Even if it is mere innocent curiosity or separation anxiety, it amounts to the same thing: a pair of wide and disconcertingly focused eyes anticipating the start of your relief. Stage fright can often occur in such pressured conditions. I often end up having to call the whole thing off, returning when I can be assured of no audience.

Later in the morning, if your host should go off to work and leave you alone in the house, it is unlikely that they will take their pets with them. This means that you could suddenly become the sole custodian of cats, dogs and various other types of creatures. Animals occupying cages or tanks aren't usually an issue but cats and dogs can make you feel like an unwanted babysitter. They sit looking at you, wondering what made you so arrogant as to think you have any business being in their house, before realising that you're probably a soft touch who will easily be duped into helping them exceed their allocation of treats before haplessly allowing them to visit unchartered parts of the house.

Being left alone with pets presents you with many a conundrum if you have not received a thorough animal logistics briefing or have not been wholly attentive to the one that took place. Various critical matters are now wholly up to you. The instructions you were given about which doors you were supposed to close are now foggy at best. An animal could end up relieving itself in the wrong place whether given free run of the house or remaining imprisoned in one room. If the cat happens to go outside via an open window or door just before you leave, are you supposed to let it remain outside for the whole day or go chasing it down the street? Can it get back in? Is it supposed to go outside at all? Have you just deleted the family pet from the lives of your hosts as a final act of knuckleheadery before leaving? It could almost be considered fortunate that there is no one around to witness your hopeless guesswork at this point, although, of course, this absence of assistance is what has brought about these quandaries in the first place. It is probably safest to cancel your plans for the day and stay in the house until your host comes back.

TWENTY ONE

Showering

It might be your wish to start the new day with a shower. You may seek to do this before presenting yourself to your host so that you appear to them well-groomed and sweet-smelling. Showering as soon as you get up might also be a necessity if you have to leave early, with no opportunity for fraternising idly over the breakfast table beforehand.

If you rise from your bed and proceed straight to the bathroom without consulting anyone, there is now a lottery of opportunity. You ideally need to shower immediately, but that might be the case for someone else too. Will you be causing untold chaos to the household's morning routine if you insert yourself into what appears to be a vacant bathroom slot? Will you be making someone late for work? Will you be forcing this person to go to work odorous, or looking unkempt or unshaven? An open door to an empty bathroom in peak getting-up hours therefore poses as a dare. The other side of this anxiously tossed coin is that if your natural reticence and consideration for others prevents you from taking advantage of the open goal, your own schedule might be thrown into disarray if someone else then takes occupation of the facility. It seems scarcely imaginable that such a cut-and-thrust scenario is possible while you're still in your pyjamas, but the world takes no prisoners before 9 AM.

During a course of study in Paris, I stayed for two weeks in a house where 7:15 AM was the optimum time for showering in order to make it to class on time with maximum sleep. Any later than this and one would have had to rush. Any earlier than this and one would have been cheated out of precious minutes of rest. Unfortunately, my cohabiting classmate also realised this. As a result, our mornings always began with an unspoken competition to see who could get into the bathroom first while also hedging their bets to get in there as luxuriously late as possible.

In practice, inevitably, she wiped the floor with me every time. I would sluggishly prize myself out of bed and make for the bedroom door just in time to hear her crossing the landing and claiming occupancy of the bathroom, the lock's click seeming to cry out 'Land ahoy!' Even the way she locked the door sounded smug, crowingly followed by the running water of the shower jeering that I couldn't even take a leak until she'd done everything she wished to do in her own good time. As I was darting back to my room from my own rushed shower sometime later in a last-minute frenzy, my classmate would be sauntering cockily down the stairs on her way to public transport with each step gloating a subtle 'fuck you'. I would arrive at class breathless and perspiring and then bitterly observe her sitting up attentively in the best seat in the house while indulgantly sipping the coffee that her leisurely journey had afforded her the time to purchase. There are probably many people reading this to whom it would only have been common sense – and easily achievable – to have avoided such a scenario by getting up a bit earlier. It is highly flattering to have my work being read by such superior life forms.

Taking a shower – just as with all bathroom procedures – is such a habitual part of daily life, so ingrained and automatic, that we go through the required motions without any conscious mental effort. Our muscles remember all the stuff about how to switch the appliance on and about picking up the right cleansing products and applying them to the most appropriate parts of ourselves. Our bodies do this work while our brains get an extra few minutes of sleep, assuming we are showering in the morning. At home, the shower itself will usually be pre-set to spray us with water of our preferred temperature and pressure, so we don't need to think about that either.

There is already plenty of scope for being caught out when using the bathroom for a shorter transaction than a shower during a visit to someone else's home. You can wind up attempting to wash your hands with the lotion that has been surreptitiously positioned next to the soap. You can be soaked through by a tidal wave from an indelicately handled tap, forcing you to return to the social gathering looking like you failed to make it to the facility in time. I struggle to brush my teeth without getting white spots of toothpaste up the bathroom mirror, yet so rarely do I arrive at a pre-splattered mirror in anyone else's house that, unless no human has ever missed a bit while wiping it off, it must only be me who suffers from this foible.

Showering on unfamiliar territory, particularly during what for many – especially me – is the time of day when mental agility is at its lowest ebb, is an obstacle course of yet greater cognitive exercise than anything you are likely to be getting up to in the washbasin or lavatory. It also comes with a great deal more protocol.

Before barricading yourself hastily inside the bathroom for a shower, lured by the aforementioned open door that hopefully wasn't being eyed up by anyone who had an urgent need to use the facility before you, it is sensible to plan ahead. If you have been furnished with a towel, it is very important indeed that you remember to take this in with you. If you leave it in your bedroom but then remember about it upon reaching the bathroom, you can always go back and retrieve it but you then run the risk of an opportunist from another bedroom stealing your bathroom slot. If you get to the end of your time in the shower and only then register that the towel really ought to have come along for the ride, you are in slightly more of a pickle. You could theoretically lower your standards to the extent of chancing it with another towel already hanging in the bathroom but you probably don't want it on your conscience that you have intimately wiped yourself down with the cloth of another, even if you don't mind their DNA and goodness-knows-what-else on your own fair skin.

I once attempted to compensate for a forgotten towel, in one of my less glorious moments, by attempting to dry myself with toilet paper. In my post-shower confinement, it was the only available absorbent commodity. The said resource was of predictably pathetic durability and it stuck to me eagerly, resulting in a hopelessly extravagant paper-to-skin ratio that ended up with me looking like I'd been mummified and then caught in a downpour. Having dishonourably finished the roll before being forced to give up, I was then reduced to having to hose myself down anew in the shower before observing that the papery remnants were – not surprisingly with hindsight – clogging the plughole. For the record, I sorted it, felt ashamed of my private exhibition of low intelligence and resolved not to do anything so foolish in future.

Should you ever alight from the shower and realise that you have forgotten your own towel, it is to be assumed that your generous helpings of common sense will inspire you to dry yourself with the clothes that you wore on entry to the bathroom. This was my course of action some years ago when getting ready before a wedding although, regrettably, while desperately gasping for early morning brain power, I caught myself getting dried with the ironed shirt that I had been about to put on for the day. It is to be hoped that the common sense that inspired you to dry yourself with clothes in the absence of a towel – and ideally reminded you to avoid using the day's formalwear for the purpose –will not have allowed you to have scampered from the bedroom to the bathroom in an indecent state. Such foolhardy behaviour would, in addition to placing to your modesty in obvious danger, cause you not to have any garments to hand for emergency drying purposes. In the event of having forgotton your towel while taking such a gamble, you would have to resort to drip-drying via naked and energetic laps of the bathroom.

If you haven't been given a towel and there is no one around who might be able to provide one, you might have to do a tasteful amount of digging. If there exists what is *obviously* an airing cupboard on your flight path to the showering facility, this could well be where the towels are kept and you could gingerly extract one on your way past. If you are me, which admittedly you are almost certainly not, there is a good chance of ending up with the towel that only the dog uses and subsequently emerging from the shower with a somewhat hairier appearance and texture than before.

It never pays to assume that a towel left in the bathroom is for your benefit, even if only one person lives in the house and has told you that they shower in their en-suite. My friend once stayed with someone who, some days into the sojourn, expressed surprise upon encountering him wrapped in the towel that had been neatly folded up in the bathroom at the beginning of the visit and which my friend naïvely assumed was his. 'Mate, you've been wiping my balls on your face for the last three days!' the host exclaimed, his jollity suggesting a failure to register that the reverse also had to have been true.

If you're sorted with a towel, you can get straight on with the actual business of showering. The first thing you will need to do is work out how to make the shower enclosure as watertight as possible to minimize the aquatic devastation you could leave behind. In a shower cubicle, this is a simple case of closing the door. If the shower is suspended over a bath, the flood defences will take the form of a curtain or a slightly inadequate glass screen running halfway along the length of the bath. The latter ensures that only half of the bathroom gets irrigated. I once stayed in a house where the shower was attached to a very elegant freestanding bath with no curtain. It was as if guests were positively encouraged to drench the place. Were one to sit down? I ended up doing so but it was logistically compromising, being somewhat of a challenge to access certain areas in this manner, and the floor still ended up looking like the scene of a firefighters' training exercise.

If you find yourself in a curtained setup, I'm sure it goes without saying to one as quick-witted and worldly as you that you will need to ensure that the curtain is tucked inside the bath. A lot of shower curtains rejoice in coming open at the other end when you've pulled them all the way across, so perhaps check for that as well.

Once you've got a shower curtain under control so that it does its job, you will then find that it develops a persistent and irritating physical attraction to you while you're attempting to get washed. There is still no concrete scientific theory as to why or how this happens. The running shower water causes the curtain to be blown – or sucked – in, creating a potentially claustrophobic situation for the soapy customer. A variety of possible explanations exists for this phenomenon, of which one of the most commonly cited is *Bernoulli's Principle.*

Daniel Bernoulli was a Dutch-born mathematician and physicist in the eighteenth century who spent most of his working life in Switzerland, some years before he'd be called upon to explain why millions of people around the world battled each morning with a sheet of damp canvas adhering to their buttocks, a phenomenon that he would probably not have experienced himself. He was from a family of similarly brainy individuals, with his father, Johann, being one of the early developers of Calculus. Johann, having raised a son of immense intellect and acclaim, couldn't quite reconcile his ego with coming joint first with Daniel in a Parisian scientific competition and so banned his child from the family home. If ever there was a man who deserved to be painted into a corner of scalding water by a shower curtain it must surely have been Johann, although he wouldn't have known why it was happening.

Anyhow, Daniel elucidates in his 1738 book *Hydrodynamica,* plagiarised by his ever-supportive father, that air pressure drops as fluid speeds up. Thus, an imbalance of air pressure is created when the shower starts to run because the pressure inside the shower is lower than the pressure outside. This causes the higher-pressure air outside the curtained enclosure to push in against the curtain and thus towards the person attempting to hose themselves down while standing inside the area of lower pressure. However, a gentleman called David Schmidt performed an experiment in 2001 to show that the droplets of water from the shower create a sideways vortex thanks to their deceleration transferring energy to the area around the bathtub. I am conscious that none of this academia will be of any comfort or fascination when you're bollock-naked and covered in suds first thing in the morning, unable to get the water temperature to exceed freezing yet equally powerless to detach the curtain from your area. It is probably astute to carry a brick in your overnight bag with which to hold the curtain down. It's probably even more astute not to reveal that you do so.

It is also important to prepare the vicinity of the shower for your disembarking, as you would at home, both for your comfort and so that the next person to use the bathroom doesn't need to wear wellies. You will lay out the ensemble of bathmats and towels provided, which will protect your feet from cold-induced startlement and also hopefully soak up the flood created from the shower while your concentration is diverted in scholarly wonder towards the work of Bernoulli and Schmidt, to whom your naked commemoration in this setting would probably come as at least a mild surprise. Now that the harbour is prepared, it is time to climb aboard and attempt a command of the shower's controls.

Some years ago, if you'll forgive this momentary tangent, my friend picked his car up from the garage and later spent an exercised fifteen minutes ranting to me about how the mechanic had had the moronic indecency to move the seat. I struggled to understand the problem.

'Will it not go back?' I asked, attempting to tune my compassion to his wavelength.

'You don't need to move a seat to change a headlight bulb,' he fulminated, not one bit suspicious of the disproportion of his indignation. 'It took me hours to get it back to how I like it.'

My eyes now abruptly torn open to the anality of others, I was mortified to think of the dozens of times I had handed appliances or other items back to their owners with their configurations subtly or even drastically adapted to my preferences. I had previously had no idea that people were so profoundly incapable of restoring their devices to their preferred settings without hours of aggrieved measurement, or indeed that such things as the driver's seat's proximity to the pedals had ever been the summation of hours of precise calculation in the first place. A horrifying mental catalogue of faux pas on my part, spanning many years, now edged into focus. I'd watched people's televisions and switched them off without reverting to the channel from which I had flicked away. I'd used people's toasters and forgotten to restore their preferred level of toastiness after use. Come to that, I'd borrowed cars and moved the seat so that I could either reach the pedals or ensure a situation where I wasn't driving with my knees around my ears. I had almost certainly, therefore, adjusted the water temperature on someone's shower and overlooked the need to return it to how I'd found it. Rendered speechless by the newfound and tragic extent to which I was a thoughtless dickhead, I marvelled introspectively at the fact that I had any friends left at all.

If you have a friend whose disposition makes you suspect that they'd be unlikely to cope with a mechanic adjusting a car seat in order to drive the vehicle safely, this friend almost certainly won't want you trifling with the configurations of temperature and water flow in their shower. I would tentatively advise you to do so anyway, however, as it might do them good to be reminded that disaster can strike at any time.

Before you can feel so pampered as to be adjusting things to your precise requirements, you will need to work out how on earth one extracts any water from the contraption in the first place. I'm sure many of you will never have had any difficulty in this regard and indeed may not have experienced any of the potential house-guest hazards exposed since the beginning of this book. Being of above-average fallibility, however, I feel a duty to assist the ill-fated minority. These are my people.

An electric shower will either trickle or gush to life at the touch of a button. If it doesn't, there will probably be a cord on the other side of the room that you need to pull. Very occasionally, it will be a button on the other side of the bathroom door instead, in which case it's prudent to be at least partially covered before leaving the room to press it unless you're feeling particularly edgy or immodest. Piloting an unfamiliar power shower will involve much more vagueness and trial-and-error as you inquisitively and slightly nervously twist taps and knobs while waiting for something to happen.

In either case, eventual mastery of the system is confirmed with a sudden release of water that will either scald you or strike you with a blast so icy that your testicles themselves – if indeed you are fitted with such things – may let out an audible shriek. Furthermore, there is no guarantee as to the source of the initial splash. If the shower is over the bath and connected to the taps, there is somehow a default setting for the water to emerge from the taps to fill the bath, even if no one has intentionally specified this option for two years.

After this unexpected spurt of blisteringly hot or cold water has playfully splashed your foot and caused you to bash your leg on the tap in alarm, you will need to play around with a little knob above the tap to divert the water through the showerhead. The setup can sneak back into bath mode at will: a little knob indeed. Exceptionally fancy people sometimes have two showerheads in the same cubicle and I have no idea why. There is no telling which one will emit water. Sometimes, the showerhead has been left facing in an unwise direction, causing you to take urgent action when it fires up and pressure-washes the room.

Owing to the opening temperature being unpalatable, it is necessary to let the shower run for a minute while things settle down. While this process is unfolding in the shower at home, one instinctively knows where to stand and how to order the doors and curtains. When showering in an unknown region, however, the shower cubicle can turn into a thirty-second torture chamber at this point as you are held up against the wall by the onslaught of blisteringly hot or heart-stoppingly cold water. Alternatively, you might escape the pain of extreme water temperatures by stepping out of the enclosure. This may transform the bathroom into a small boating lake because it will require you to open the shower door or curtain.

When the temperature settles down, you can start experimenting with different intensities of water flow and heat but you will probably wish you hadn't bothered because everything will inexplicably turn stone-cold, unbearably hot or reduce to a trickle and it will be impossible to retrieve the tolerable setting with which you started. You will be covered in a lather of soap by this point and feeling mildly anxious about how you're going to rinse yourself down. As with all technology, 'turning it off and on again' can solve things, at least with an electric shower, although you might still emerge from the shower afflicted by the idiosyncratic combination of hypothermia and third-degree burns. Attempts to adjust the water-jet settings on the shower head will see the whole thing coming apart in your hand, so it's probably best to contain your curiosity with that. Your host would surely ask why you hadn't asked for help at the time if you were to recount to them your time on this battlefield of aquatic discomfort but, when you're standing there naked and foamy, you don't always feel like involving a third party.

I am never sure of the etiquette concerning the use of a host's toiletries. It would be a little unusual to bring one's own soap to a dinner party to wash one's post-lavatorial hands, so why might it be irreverent to help oneself to the body and hair potions of others? It is normal to travel with a wash bag containing shampoo and so forth but is this custom born out of a social consensus to use our own consumables or is it for the rather more self-centred reason that our hosts may not possess our favourite products?

I suppose many variables influence whether we use the toiletries in other people's showers, such as the intimacy of the acquaintance and whether the products lined up are the supermarket's own brand (probably okay to help yourself) or your host's dainty and luxurious Christmas presents that cost £42.85 for 100ml (best leave these alone). Whether or not it's officially the done thing to use these things, will anyone even know? If I, a strapping alpha male who only last Saturday evening sank almost two cans of Brewdog Punk India Pale Ale, were to emerge from the bathroom in a fragrant haze of geranium and ninja-berry, maybe someone would suspect. In any case, I always take my own shampoo, shower gel and macho facewash when staying away from home. I was much less careful about taking shower gel before the time I forgot to top up my supply and was greeted in a shower – routinely used by several people – by one solitary bar of soap, the anatomical adventures of which didn't bear thinking about. In many showers, one might also encounter soft and semi-absorbent hanging items that defy description. I *know* you don't touch those.

If you decide to go ahead with the products left in the shower and you have anything less than 20/20 vision, it is sensible to wear your glasses or other sight-correcting apparatus while making your selection. Some hosts, particularly where the showering space is confined and lacks storage solutions, leave cleaning products about the place. Where this is the case, sleepiness combined with impaired vision could lead you to bathe yourself in a froth of Windowlene or burn off your unmentionables with bleach. A relative of mine used to keep vinegar in the bathroom for cleaning purposes, which led to a long-sighted guest emerging from the shower smelling for all the world like a portion of chips. A similar incident saw someone vowing to think twice in future before applying a host's aerosol deodorant without reading the label, as he confidently started the day with a bountiful cloud of Glade Floral Blossom under each armpit.

Once you're done in the shower, it's important to think about your journey back to your sleeping quarters. If you're of bodily confidence or well acquainted with your host, you could simply exit the room wrapped in your towel, assuming you remembered it. For this to be a success, the towel needs to be of a size with plenty of built-in margin for error, lest anything tries to poke out for some sun or you happen to walk past the source of a breeze. You could alternatively wear your pyjamas, of course. You could even get dressed for the day in the bathroom if you have gone in with the requisite resources. This is recommended if you are sleeping in a communal area because it could transpire that the room is no longer your sanctuary when you emerge from the bathroom.

I knew a chap who slept the night, unplanned and unannounced to most of the resident family, in the living room of a vicarage after a night out. His friend was a vicar's son. The man chanced it with modesty and scuttled back from the shower to the living room in a skimpy towel, which he discarded as soon as he crossed the threshold and felt secure once more in the privacy of the room in which he had been sleeping. Regrettably, he then turned around in a somewhat bare condition to the sight of the bishop sitting in a purple cassock on the very sofa where the gentleman had been sleeping only an hour earlier. Everyone concerned reportedly turned the same shade as the cassock while the conversation between the bishop and vicar stopped in its tracks, as indeed did both their hearts. A couple of nonagenarian nuns subsequently filed into the room for what was a long-standing ecclesiastical engagement. The scene now combined elements of a hen party and a funeral, the latter now threatening to be an imminent reality for at least one of the nuns. The vicar's wife, unaware of the bare visitor, called through from the kitchen and asked if anyone wanted cocktail sausages, to which the bishop attempted to diffuse the situation by responding that there was already one being presented in the living room.

TWENTY TWO

Leaving the Bathroom as You Found It

I always feel a firm obligation to leave a bathroom precisely as I found it. Of course, it would be a touch impertinent by any standards for me to vacate the family's facilities having smashed the tiles up and left my underwear lying around. Nonetheless, I am perhaps a touch over-punctilious about appearing housetrained, going to great pains to leave people's bathrooms bearing as little account as possible of my visit.

I'm not sure why I impose such severe conditions on myself because I don't tend to stay with people who are terribly highly strung and I haven't taken offence when guests have left their mark on my own amenities. I have variously hosted friends who have presumed that the shower curtain was something merely laid on as an optional extra for the agoraphobic, friends who have taken advantage of my most expensive aftershave and a friend with the peculiarly intimate trait of leaving behind a signature pair of Y-fronts – each a different earth tone – at the end of each stay as a sort of elasticated calling card. This is to say nothing of guests who have left the taps running or those who liked to leave the bathroom light on all night so that the window could act as a beacon for passing aircraft.

All these trivial grumbles are, of course, eclipsed a hundredfold by the priceless joy that the company of these rare and delightful people bestows upon my home and my life. One cannot beat the cherished memories created or the first-rate banter generated between oneself and the lovable souls for whom one has unhesitatingly flung wide one's palace gates. Even in the aforementioned cases of people bringing their alternative interpretations of domestic protocol to the party, the friendships have only been strengthened by the time spent together. This is not least in the case of Mr Undergarments, who has now stayed enough times for me to have amassed the resources to construct – should ever the need arise – a lengthy and durable string of camouflage bunting. However, I still proceed with caution as a guest in case my hosts are not quite as unconditionally zen as I am.

One of the first pangs of self-consciousness to strike me after a shower in someone else's house is brought on by having drenched the bathroom with steam. This is fairly easily avoided if staying in a modern property with an extractor fan – although even then one is likely to leave an ambiguously damp toilet roll and be unable to use the mirror for some time afterwards unless a squeegee is kicking around – but what if no such ventilating commodity exists? Some bathrooms get so damagingly soaked that one wonders if one has missed an obvious precaution, or simply been in there too long.

I once stayed in an old house in which the elderly proprietor's habitat was an aesthetically perpetual 1968, where screaming floral wallpaper in the bathroom had been approved some decades ago in a move that was as misguided as a visual enhancement as it was as a practical wall-covering for a room hosting wet and steamy events on a daily basis. I stood in the pale-blue bath, over which was suspended a showerhead, and tampered with the taps until the rickety and asthmatic shower eventually wheezed to life and let out a trickle of water. The parsimonious water outlet took a while to dampen me thoroughly but this inconvenience was surpassed when, after a little while, I noticed that the abundance of steam appeared to be causing the oversized marigold motif adorning the wall to bubble and peel. I couldn't have been the first person to have aggravated this decay but I felt certain that I was somehow abusing the delicate and venerable facilities. It seemed counter-intuitive to open the frosted window as the rain was pounding heavily but, out of desperation to ventilate the room and save the wallpaper, I artlessly tugged at the sash adjacent to the bath and hoisted it up. The window's proximity to a bus queue resulted in yet another of the limitless opportunities for inadvertent public nudity that so regularly and predictably seem to present themselves on unfamiliar premises.

Similar to steam damage is the scenario where the water from the shower cannot be contained in the enclosure despite your best efforts. The fabric of the room must go through this every day and withstand it but sometimes it's easy to feel like you've vandalised the joint.

Some people like to apply aftershave, aerosol deodorant and other such fragrant products in the bathroom after a shower. This is all perfectly sensible if applied in moderation, although it's probably nice for your host to be able to breathe when they go in there themselves. Hosts sometimes keep fine aftershave in the bathroom, of which I'm pretty sure it's not the done thing to avail oneself without permission – hence my mentioning people doing so moments ago. I once came across a bottle of aftershave in someone's bathroom that was identical to the one I'd brought along myself. I was reluctant even to use my own, lest my smelling of it projected the impression that I'd helped myself to that of my host.

What should you do with your used towel? This is an undiscussed grey area. It being a bathroom item, you might naturally feel it right to anchor your towel in there after use but there is often more to it than that. What if there's no space for it? What if there's nowhere to put it that *absolutely* differentiates it from the towels of the permanent residents? This is not an issue if you've been given a towel that contrasts wildly with the family's matching ensemble of towels that was purchased to complement the decor. However, if you've been given a towel that looks like everyone else's and you then go mindlessly tossing yours in near the others, your host may be reduced to washing the lot to avoid the possibility of a family member defiling themselves with the DNA of the character who set the burglar alarm off en route to the WC. I once stayed with a family that was very into its designer labels and the towels reflected this. They had made a good compromise between style and substance – we all had white towels so as not to cause visual dissonance but I had a different designer label to everyone else. I believe mine was 'Hilton' and theirs were all 'Ibis'. They were very durable indeed.

The other option is to leave the towel in your room, which is perfectly workable in a bedroom with an accessible radiator but less so if sleeping in a communal area. Putting one's bath towel on the living room radiator doesn't always seem like the hallmark of an unobtrusive house guest, while the electric heaters found in some properties carry strict admonishments that they should not be covered. These rules are probably worth obeying if it means nobody burns alive, although your towel would at least dry out with record-breaking efficiency if the worst came to the worst. If you are departing and there's nowhere obvious to leave your wet towel, it's probably okay to leave it on top of your bedding since it will all be washed anyway but the contact between wet and dry linen always feels somewhat dissonant to me. I'd suggest bringing dry shampoo and paper towels to eliminate the dilemma but I have a niggling suspicion that no one else actually cares.

Even toilet rolls harbour risks of predicament. Many households have a wall-mounted or freestanding toilet roll holder that doesn't cause any problems but sometimes one might encounter a situation where the toilet roll is unanchored and unenclosed, perhaps perched upon the pedestal or a nearby windowsill. These things can be surprisingly lively. I was once in a toilet cubicle in a department store when an unravelling toilet roll hurtled past my feet from next door and proceeded with some urgency through – presumably – the entire row, forming a white paper barrier that appeared to be trying to cordon off the occupants in the manner of police tape. The consternation of my neighbours, as this unstoppable two-ply runaway train shot past them at such close quarters during their private endeavours, can only be imagined. One expects a more serene pace of life in such an environment.

If one is careless enough to let go of a free-range bog roll in the context of someone's home, perhaps when lifting it down from a surface above the pedestal or while tearing a piece off and overlooking the need to keep hold of the body of the thing, there is a fair chance of dropping it down the toilet. It is important not to do this because it certainly doesn't work as well after being recovered from such a wet and unsterile abyss. When your host finds out what you've done, either via your confessing or upon their discovering the soggy item in the bin, it hardly promotes you as a dependable pair of hands. I recently visited a friend and found the toilet roll sitting snugly atop the warm bathroom radiator, heated for use – the ultimate creature comfort on a winter's day. However, the possibility now occurs to me that it could have been in this position because it was drying out from an incident such as I describe.

Even the disposal of toilet paper can be a minefield if you are travelling abroad. There are parts of the world where is it not acceptable to send it on its journey via the lavatory at all and a bin is therefore provided. Even where it is indeed flushed away after use, there can be delicate considerations.

My friend and I once stayed in a tiny and venerable apartment in Barcelona, where the proprietor told us that if we flushed more than five sheets of toilet paper down at once, it would clog up the antiquated plumbing system for the entire building. I wryly asked him whether, if I were to use only four sheets in my first flush, it might be acceptable to carry the fifth sheet over to the next transaction and thus flush six down the following time. This drew one of the very blankest looks I have ever seen, to be followed by my friend profusely apologising to the man for my existence. The stay there taught me not to be too indulgent with the stuff, which is a useful discipline when using a facility where the toilet roll is getting towards the end and there are no spares in sight.

It is something of a faux pas to leave a bathroom without any toilet roll remaining – assuming of course that the bathroom features a toilet – and so I ration myself carefully if it looks like I'm going to be forced into this position. Leaving the toilet roll with one sheet left so that you haven't technically finished it exhibits a calculated laziness and your host will probably know what you're up to. If possible, therefore, it's probably best to leave at least a complete rotation's worth behind.

Once you've finished agonising over the toilet roll protocol (assuming you'd started) and added some paper to the contents of the lavatory, you will of course expel these contents from the premises via a hearty flush, if you're in a country where this is acceptable. If the prospect of being disturbed in the bathroom can make the heart jump, there is little in these surroundings that can make the heart sink quite like when a flush of the toilet results in a blockage. The water level rises to just below the bowl's rim like a vertical tide coming in, the solids either floating to the surface or remaining wedged in the porcelain bottleneck through which they were supposed to take leave. You are then encumbered with a deep sense of responsibility for clearing the blockage, in addition to a feeling of impending unease when you consider that it might not be possible to do this without any tools at your disposal.

If such a blockage has occurred and you are now anxiously pondering the way forward, it is carried unanimously between you and perhaps a watchful pumice stone that the situation could be considered at least mildly embarrassing. It is easy to take things personally and develop a complex centred on this unromantic aspect of human existence, apropos of which you might previously have had no cause to be anything but bold and confident.

You might previously have eliminated waste with an almost arrogant abandon, forcing the lavatory to take it and deal with it while you brazenly walked away – practically a hit-and-run scenario. Now, however, it is as if the toilet has actually rejected your offering. This is a low blow by any measure. The implication is that your excreta is so obscenely fierce in both volume and robustness that a standard domestic WC could not possibly be expected to accommodate it. You should have offloaded it in the field or in a corner of your stable, it seems to be saying.

As the minutes expire in tandem with your credibility, an emotionally destructive thought process might be taking root. You might now suspect that a crisis of this nature has never previously unfolded in this particular bathroom. Surely people couldn't live with this happening regularly. It would be easy to arrive at the unflattering conclusion that while your host's turds are chic and dainty, posing no challenge to the plumbing, yours are thunderous and unwieldy by comparison. You don't want your host to be made aware of this unattractive truth and so will do everything possible to avoid an exposé of your waste products being incompatible with the parameters of the family privy. It is also rather in the spirit of leaving things as you found them for there not to be an aquarium of stools and saturated paper greeting your host when they next rock up there in response to the call of nature.

In truth, there isn't always a huge amount you can do in this situation and I'm not sure you want to be reading about the possibilities anyway, particularly if you're eating lunch. Ideally, unless you've deposited something of such majestic substance as to be of potential interest to the Forestry Commission, the lavatorial water level should at least start to fall and thus reduce the visual impact of what has occurred. It is tempting to flush again under the illusion that everything will work out the second time but this is more likely to set you back to the beginning of the ordeal, often resulting in the waterline rising more precariously close to the point of overflowing than before. If all this is playing out during the day and you have just nipped out of the living room to relieve yourself while your host awaits your return downstairs to continue with the tea and shortbread, a realisation on your part of the amount of time you've now been missing starts to add to the anxiety. Defeated, your only option might be just to return to your host and gingerly offer something along the lines of 'your toilet seems to be blocked,' in an unconvincingly detached register that attempts to transfer the responsibility from you to the lavatory itself. This will fool no one and will probably paint a wholly accurate picture of what has actually happened.

A further way of disgracing ourselves in other people's bathrooms is by breaking things. This is a particular speciality of mine. I don't do it in an iconoclastic sort of way, ungratefully assaulting the ceramics with a mallet, but I often seem to disturb latent vulnerabilities with the fittings. This has frequently led to my having to complete a DIY project before vacating, in order to leave no record of my inadvertent vandalism. Other people's bathrooms are full of such pitfalls. One example is the towel rail that jumps off the wall if you pull the towel more than a centimetre towards you, with the installation then landing in more pieces than you realised it comprised and which resist the floor tiles with a loud clatter. Presumably, this is a sort of primitive alarm system to stop people from stealing the towels. The list goes on: light-cord handles that come off in your hand, shower heads that detach from the hose but devoutly refuse to go back on again (begging the question of how these things are made in the first place) and shower curtains that come off the runners. It is just as well that the door is usually locked and I can therefore carry out the repairs without the possibility of someone walking in, although a piece of metal crashing onto a tiled bathroom floor can sometimes arouse the concern of a host.

I don't think I am terribly heavy-handed and so, if something breaks on me during a bathroom visit, I try telling myself that it must have been in some way faulty or fragile to start with. In a state of mild disquiet, I find myself wondering if it's the first time the incident has occurred and I truly have broken whatever it may be, or if I'm just uninitiated with regard to the booby traps.

I recently came a cropper on a relative's toilet seat (a cropper on a crapper, you might say) when said seat transpired not to be bolted to the porcelain. Inevitably, this shortcoming caused my unsuspecting backside to cave into the receptacle with an exhilarating zip at a moment when I'd have preferred stability and comfort. Putting aside the indignity of it all and my present palpitations, I had now effectively broken the toilet seat. My pride had accompanied me down the lavatory and a difficult conversation seemed imminent. Had this throne been defective before my ascension to it?

I took mental stock of the regular users of the facility and realised at once that the seat had frequently been sat on by heavier people than me. Still, it was during my transaction that the incident had occurred and so I felt it was up to me to fix it. I spent some time faffing around with the defunct hinges and clips before lining the thing up correctly so that it functioned and opened and closed as if I'd never been there. Indeed, I believed I'd effected an improvement as the accessory now seemed at least notionally secured to the toilet. I contentedly departed the scene feeling satisfied with my craftsmanship but, fifteen minutes later, there was a loud expression of surprise from the bathroom as the seat capsized anew and its next victim plummeted buttock-first into the bowl. The shriek occasioned those resident to exchange heated remarks about how this terrifying posterior trap had been awaiting repair for many weeks and how it was everyone else's fault that the task remained outstanding. No matter: I was a mere casualty. I breathed a sigh of relief while some poor soul behind a locked door flailed around helplessly with their feet in the air and their bottom wedged inside a ceramic entrapment.

Fortunately, not all bathroom breakages are so pulsatingly lethal but we still fear the reprisals even if we're not being directly injured via the mishap. I once stayed with a lady who was a keen cyclist and whose bathroom sported a unique free-standing toilet roll holder made from bicycle components. She told me proudly that it had been specially made for her by a former boyfriend. I couldn't be sure whether it remained in situ as a monument to a sadly missed relationship or if an altogether different set of sentiments was being expressed via its duty as a toilet roll holder. In any case, she was extremely attached to the item, as indeed was the toilet roll when I arrived. However, in the middle of the night, it was incumbent upon me to change the roll. I could – and should – have innocently left it to my host to sort out the next day but I wanted to seem thoughtful and mechanically intelligent. I unscrewed a bolt that I thought would release the toilet roll but which instead, regrettably, released another piece of metal to the tiled floor with a deafening report. The success of the operation continued at that rate, with the creation ending up pretty well reduced to component form, before my attempts to reconstruct it produced something that resembled a bicycle more closely than it did a toilet roll holder. This could have been useful because, by that point, I just wanted to ride away into the night. Thankfully, in a state of high tension, I managed to reassemble the thing in accordance with a photograph I had taken earlier – with my host's permission – for the benefit of a cycling-enthused friend.

My experiences in my own home tell me that, however responsible you feel for triggering a dysfunction with the bathroom furnishings, your host is usually already aware of the issue. Some years ago, my bathroom sported a door handle that came off each time one pulled it shut, which was rather boring but I honed a technique to navigate the inadequacy without having to get involved in the business of repairing it. Every time anyone visited, there would be a loud crash as the pieces of door handle fell to the floor, followed by a long period of quiet restoration as the person attempted to reattach it before coming to tell me that the handle was broken and they had surely worsened it. I'd tell them that I knew and not to worry. My apparent lack of a sense of urgency regarding my home's crumbling fabric typically made guests look at me like I was incapable of looking after myself. Perhaps they were on to something.

TWENTY THREE

Exiting the Bedroom

It is jolly good etiquette on departure to leave your bedroom in a condition that is as close as possible to that in which you found it. Theoretically, this shouldn't be too difficult. You arrived with a bag containing your clothes and other personal effects and you will leave with the same bag and its contents. Ideally, you will not have done anything overly drastic to your sleeping space while occupying it.

The main act of housekeeping before departure concerns the bed. I always feel it leaves a lasting impression of decency to make the bed before you leave, even though it will be stripped by your host when you've gone. It perhaps therefore demonstrates even greater thoughtfulness to strip the bed yourself before departure but it is advisable to budget extra time to make sure you complete this task in its entirety. A job half-done could convey the impression that you couldn't really be arsed. It is in the same league as leaving one solitary piece of toilet paper left on the roll. If sleeping on a sofa, I always at least *intend* to fold everything and pile it up, which typically results in the bedding occupying just as much of the sofa as before but the gesture feebly attempts to show that thought has been given.

I always feel some responsibility for the returning-to-normal of a communal space. An airbed taking up the whole living room might typically be demolished by you and your host as a joint effort in order that both parties feel like they've done their bit, although in practice this might not be required thanks to the airbed's natural overnight deflation. Sofa beds will require you both to take to YouTube to watch relevant demonstrations of their being folded up by trained professionals with intimidatingly effective biceps.

Not irrelevantly, a friend once recounted an uncomfortable episode in which he had secreted his own bedding into his friend's house owing to an apparent inability to make a comfortable nest with sheets that differed from those he used at home. This was not a man who could adapt to circumstances. Regrettably, he was as unaccustomed to stripping his bed of a morning as he was to the distressing sensation of an unfamiliar bed sheet, causing him to trot breezily off home the next day while his sheets remained installed on his host's mattress. His time spent changing the bed the night before had evidently not made a sufficiently indelible impression on his memory. He felt – and looked, one imagines – quite the twat upon returning later in the day to ask for the sheets back. If you are wont to do this sort of thing, you should also carry with you a large banner – not less than two metres wide – that you can hang in front of the bed and ideally across the door, so that you cannot physically leave the room without reading the words 'STRIP BEFORE DEPARTURE' or whatever slogan or directive will jog your memory. Unless one has a skin condition that calls for attentive measures, it is hardly a compliment to one's host's Egyptian cotton when they find their own textiles lying on the floor in place of another man's polyester, nor indeed does it flatter a host's polyester when they find it similarly discarded in favour of their guest's Egyptian cotton.

Similarly, it is probably best to reverse any modifications that you may have felt were necessary to the layout of the room so that its Feng Shui met your precise requirements or so that it attained the degree of ergonomic friendliness that you desired. The only time I slipped up in this area was when I forgot to reinstate two barstools and a mini oven that I had had to hoist atop a wardrobe in order for the room to have sufficient floor space for me to be able to put down my suitcase. My host seemed to think guests would need all the facilities of the average kitchen, dining room and bathroom to be hemmed into the four-metre-by-four-metre bedroom in order to enjoy a comfortable stay, the irony of which was that none of it left space for much of a bed. It was clear from the proprietor's affronted expression that putting two barstools and a mini oven on top of the wardrobe was officially more absurd and inappropriate than their being in the bedroom to start with and certainly more eccentric than the fact that the guest room was fitted with a dishwasher.

If you haven't brought your own bedding, which is highly likely, all that now remains is to have a good look around the room and in the wardrobes to check that you haven't left anything behind. It is of course good form not to take your host's bra home but, as we saw earlier, this can't always be helped. There is nothing wrong with blurring the line between conscientiousness and neurosis if it means that your and everyone else's underwear is in its designated place after your departure and indeed that you haven't inadvertently left anything in your wake that could compromise your credibility. The large stuffed gorilla that keeps you company under the duvet when you're away from home is all very well but you really ought to make sure that he or she gets up at the same time as you. Your social standing would be firmly at the mercy of your host's confidentiality if the gorilla were discovered enjoying an opportunistic lie-in after your departure.

Finally, for your convenience more than your dignity, it is advisable not to leave train tickets, boarding passes or your passport atop the chest of drawers or whichever 'safe place' seemed a good idea on the first night. That said, if you do, it reduces the chances of you having to suffer a night away from your gorilla.

TWENTY FOUR

Meeting your Host in the Morning

When, or indeed *if*, you and your host meet the next morning, there will be a light-hearted exchange of mutual reassurance. Your host will be keen to know that you have slept well and found everything to your utmost satisfaction. At the same time, you might be anxious to know that you didn't cause a disturbance while navigating your way to the bathroom or do anything else to have inadvertently provoked the household's ire.

The golden rule is that, however much of a sleep-deprived or nervous wreck you might be when you present yourself to your host in the morning, you should always bullshit that you have had your best night's sleep since leaving the womb. The airbed kept you supported comfortably above the floor throughout the night. The temperature in your room would have pleased Goldilocks when she trespassed on the property of the three bears. You certainly didn't hear the dog barking at 4 AM.

Consequently, even if you are bent double with back pain, are sporting severe bags under your eyes and are struggling to put sentences together, the first conversation of the new day might go something like this:

'Morning!'

'Good morning!'

'Did you sleep well?'

'Yes, thank you – like the proverbial log!'

'Oh good – hope the airbed wasn't too uncomfortable?'

'No, not at all – and at least it wasn't far to fall out!'

'And you were warm enough? I know that room can be a bit draughty but hopefully the blanket and the electric heater compensated?'

'Oh, yes thank you – I was plenty warm enough and the heater and the blanket were the perfect combination. I was able to use the latter to smother the flames when the former caught fire.'

'Oh, goodness, sorry about that. Are you sure that the blanket was okay for fighting a fire though? It's not actually a fire blanket...'

'Well actually, the blanket went up as well I'm afraid. I'm really sorry – it was entirely my fault. I just browned myself a trifle when I awoke at 1 AM in a flame-engulfed room as if I'd just regained consciousness after a nap on the Sun and so I instinctively tossed the blanket across the appliance. When the fire brigade had been out and got the fire under control, I took a taxi down to the twenty-four-hour ASDA on the other side of town to replace both the blanket and the heater. I'm afraid the blanket might be a slightly different shade of purple from the one it replaces but it's the same size. I told the firefighters not to use the siren and to creep up the stairs in silence. I do hope we didn't wake you?'

'Oh, you didn't need to go to all that trouble – I think I was probably still awake at that time anyway. It's ironic really – I took the battery out of the smoke alarm so that it wouldn't wake you up! You must be tired this morning?'

'Oh no, I got straight back to sleep. Actually, I think taking a little trip at that time did me good – there was a nice breeze without it being too chilly.'

'Oh good – as long as you're sure! And you didn't have any trouble with the lock on the bathroom door? There's a bit of a knack to it.'

'Oh no, it was a piece of cake! In fact, the firemen were able to cut me free from the bathroom when they arrived to deal with the fire – couldn't have worked out better.'

'And I hope Brian didn't pay you a visit in the night?'

'Well, I must admit I'm not used to having a python entering the room and tickling my feet with its tongue at four in the morning but honestly, it was no trouble – actually it felt like quite the novelty! My heart hadn't stopped for years so it probably did it good to have a few minutes' break.'

'Ah, yes, he often does that... Well, so long as he didn't disturb you too much. I tend to shut him downstairs at night but Tornado knows how to open the utility room door with his paws.'

'Ah yes – Tornado knows how to open *bedroom* doors too! How endearingly eccentric that German Shepherds think you'll want to play fetch at six in the morning when they climb onto the bed and drop their wet cricket balls on your head from seventy centimetres' height on the off-chance! What an adorable nocturnal double-act he and the snake make!'

'Oh goodness – he didn't?!...'

'Oh no, not last night, and if he did I slept right through it. I'm talking about Munchballs – *Chris'* German Shepherd! Staying the night in a house with another German Shepherd just reminded me.'

'Ah, phew! Coffee?'

When this conversation has taken place, your host may generously serve some breakfast or simply point out the areas of the kitchen where you are welcome to forage for some. During the consumption of this morning repast, it might be challenging to constitute what might be considered dynamic company if you are not a morning person. My personality does not light up the room in the mornings. Indeed, now I come to reflect, it could be argued that this shortcoming extends into the afternoons and evenings, but I am reputed in my social circles for being particularly poor company at breakfast time. People who know me well don't tend to expend much time or energy on attempting to interact with me first thing in the morning, dully aware from previous experience that their investment will yield an unsatisfying return. Someone with whom I am staying, on the other hand, might already have been on the go for many hours and washed the car, written a book or conceived a child. I pride myself on offering such people the opportunity to look virtuous.

Since my ambitions during that part of the day are as modest as my capabilities are limited. I am usually left alone to sip coffee and scowl in the corner until I've mellowed a bit and assembled the brainpower to identify the most appropriate utensil for spreading the butter on my toast. Indeed, my first challenge in this area used to be making sure I poured my coffee into the most suitable item of crockery but I have been less precious about this since the morning I arrived downstairs in a house in France to the sight of everyone drinking black coffee out of bowls. These days, therefore, if I drowsily pour my coffee into my cereal bowl, I can pass it off as a deliberate act of continental sophistication. This is so long as I don't mind the inevitable flip side that is having to then eat my cornflakes out of the adjacent saucer-mounted cup. All this optimistically assumes that I poured the coffee first and did not wind up adding it to some pre-decanted cereal that was in the bowl already. It is remarkable that I passed my driving test on the first attempt, although perhaps I would not be in a position to be making this minor boast if the test had taken place before mid-afternoon.

One of the more novel – indeed, sometimes mildly frightening – aspects of seeing your host first thing in the morning is the possibility of encountering them in a more primitive state of appearance than you ever have done previously. They might be wearing an outrageous dressing gown, perhaps a kimono like that of *Coronation Street's* Ken Barlow.

Entirely incidentally, Ken's kimono once reportedly ended up costing the *Corrie* team twenty-five thousand pounds. It was decided in the interests of audience decency to re-shoot several scenes when it came to light that the garment was so short as to have exposed Mr Barlow's danglers in a scene where he was being filmed from below while walking down the stairs – a balls-up indeed. One does wonder why he didn't wear underpants, however primitive, since it was merely acting. Still, this could be another new facet of your host to which you could fatally be introduced first thing in the morning, should they be sporting a similarly undependable garment, but I do hope not because things probably wouldn't be quite the same again.

You might alternatively encounter your host without teeth, wearing curlers, or, perhaps most arrestingly in some cases, without make-up. This is a big one. I had a good friend who wore a very impressive composition of make-up every day, whether or not she planned to leave the house. On one occasion when we had arranged to spend the day together, I arrived at her house at the appointed time – quite an achievement for me – and sat waiting for her in the car as was our standard protocol. Despite my messages to say I'd arrived, she failed to materialise. Eventually, she told me via a text message to wait where I was, saying that she'd be there shortly but was 'having an emergency'. I started to worry and asked if she needed help. She insisted that she didn't. The emergency transpired to have been that she'd left her make-up bag at work the previous evening and her face was now therefore entirely undisguised. It occurred to me that I had never previously seen her without make-up in all the years we had been friends. To suddenly see someone in their organic morning mode can be like seeing them in fancy dress. In some cases, it could even be a startling change to see someone without their glasses, although of course it stands to reason that they might well not see you.

You might be joined the next morning by a cast of people who did not present themselves the night before. These could be people you know well or people you have never met. Unless your host is in the reputed habit of serving breakfast to the wider community or merely has a penchant for leaving the front door open, these people will typically be other members of the household. As discussed much earlier, they are effectively your hosts as well because you are drawing breath in their living space, even if they are not as actively involved in your residency as the person who invited you. Even I can just about lay on an early-morning display of affability and gratitude towards these people. After all, they have consented, even if reluctantly, to a near-stranger roaming around their home. Said stranger could potentially have put extra strain on the bathroom schedule or taught profane vocabulary to the family budgie. At the very least, the stranger might now be occupying the wrong seat at the breakfast table, causing everyone else to reposition politely from their habitual seating places and spend the first hour of the day feeling disorientated in their own kitchen.

The extra people might well be your host's immediate family members. It could even be that the opportunity to be introduced to the family is part of the reason for your visit, so you will likely be on your best and most attentive behaviour. You will go the extra mile to avoid making a cock of yourself or doing anything that others could find alarming or uncouth. However, there is no guarantee that this level of circumspection will be matched by the very people you are seeking not to unsettle.

Time with someone's family can sometimes make you understand the person better and help you build an appreciation of the foundations of their foibles. Alternatively, it can make you wonder how the hell they turned out as normally as they did. At any rate, you will usually find that time spent cohabiting with another family broadens the mind. I remember, a few years ago, drinking wine with a friend in his kitchen late one night when his brother, aged approximately twenty-five, entered the room wearing nothing but the skimpiest florescent green briefs I had ever seen. I initially interpreted his bold continuation into the room as the styling out of an error of judgment after he had assumed that everyone else was either out or asleep, but he subsequently acknowledged us and set about making a cup of tea. He proceeded to waltz in and out of the room in this economical state of apparel for a couple of hours. Entirely his prerogative in his own home, of course, but I think I might have worn slightly more if it had been me, especially in November.

Despite my best efforts, my unreplenishable shortage of vivacity in the morning puts me at a slight disadvantage where making a good first impression on new people is concerned, although perhaps my emotional literacy faces an unfair challenge when the range of possible new acquaintances extends to those who might introduce themselves to me attired in nothing more than their green underpants. Looking back on that episode, it is perhaps a compliment that the pants were all that the gentleman had had time to put on before the excitement of meeting me provoked his legs into spontaneously hurrying him into the room without further ado, but that theory is probably bollocks – and I suspect bollocks of a greater magnitude than anything that was being concealed by the featured undergarments. It's unlikely that I'd know what to say in such a situation at eight in the morning, but would I be any more verbally innovative at eight in the evening? I certainly struggled after midnight. In some ways I am an even less safe pair of conversational hands over breakfast with people I know than with those I am meeting for the first time, owing to the treacherous combination of misfiring early-morning thought processes and an absence of the introspective guardedness that one naturally employs when attempting not to alienate new people.

An overnight stay is often the occasion on which you meet your host's partner for the first time. For some years, I had only ever met my friend's other half at the extreme ends of the day, when I was sleeping on their sofa. The lady of the house and I would encounter each other last thing at night when she was ready for bed and then first thing in the morning when we were both still in our tasteful night attire. On the last such visit, she was heading out to work very early in the morning and I was very lucky that they both gave me the benefit of the doubt when I dozily but innocently greeted her with the observation that it was the first time we'd met when she'd been fully dressed.

TWENTY FIVE

Departure

By the time you're dressed and ready to start the new day, you have navigated the peril and puzzlement that come with being an overnight guest. The usual daytime dynamic is now restored between you and your host. Of course, you might have woken everyone up during the night by accidentally shining torches into their bedrooms, demolishing ornaments on the landing or leaving taps running. You might have trodden on the dog's foot and provoked two hours of aggrieved barking. In exceptionally wild circumstances, you might have triggered an evacuation of the premises. Builders might be anticipated at the house later in the day to provide estimates for the rebuilding of the quarter of the top floor that got lavishly singed courtesy of the electrical fire you managed to start when trying to avoid freezing to death. These possibilities taken into account, by morning, your host might well not be speaking to you at all.

However you managed to conduct yourself, the point remains that the night is dealt with and you've emerged on the other side. If your host is present, the situation now is no different from if you were just visiting for the day. You and your host might now be going out for the day or doing something similarly jolly together. Alternatively, you might simply say your goodbyes when the time comes, embrace ceremoniously and be waved off in a spirit of cordial appreciation of a time well spent. What you get up to past this point is beyond the scope of this book.

Still *within* the scope of this book, however, and threatening a further whirlwind of uncertainty, is the potential situation where your host might need to leave you to your own devices in the house before you've properly got going for the day. Your host may need to go to work early in the morning – or merely go for a long walk at dawn to get away from you as soon as possible. In more extreme cases, your host might be leaving so early that they suggest you say your official farewells the previous evening, meaning that you will wake up completely alone in the house some hours after they have vacated. It might alternatively be that you are left alone in the house after sluggishly waking up and hazily bidding your industrious friend goodbye in your pyjamas.

I always feel somewhat slovenly and unenterprising when still half-asleep and covered by blankets on my friend's sofa while he is leaving his apartment at 7 AM for a day of high-flying and handsomely paid boffinry. He typically bustles about with a cheer and vigour that contrasts vividly with my drowsy purposelessness. My intellectual capacity on waking is just about sufficient to take stock of and curtail any overflow of night-time saliva, but not always entirely effectively. My friend, on the other hand, can express himself with eloquence and wit and imagines it a worthwhile endeavour to attempt to converse with me as I lie there non-verbally and wear an unpromisingly vacant expression. He does exercises and fills a Tupperware box with some concoction of blended 'superfoods' that will make him live to be a hundred and seventy-four. One reason for his early morning energy could be that he's had a good night's sleep, not having had to go in search of coins in order to access his lavatory.

There is an initial feeling of novelty when alone in someone else's house. It's a compliment for one thing – nobody would allow you to roam around their home unaccompanied if they thought you were an unscrupulous moron. Your host might have a comfier sofa than you, a larger television or a nice piano and you can luxuriate in the joy of all these things as if they were your own. Eventually, however, there is an overwhelming sense of responsibility. What if the phone rings? This isn't a very likely scenario in this day and age where landline use has sharply declined but, if it does happen, there's still the sense that one should do something despite not knowing quite what. You can answer it and not really know what to say or you can *not* answer it and be forced to hear the caller divulge intimate confidences to the answer machine, under the illusion that they are addressing an empty house. A largely obsolete concern though, as I say.

It is not just the phone that might require you to think on your feet. A parcel could arrive – a very important parcel – and it will be up to you to find the front door key, negotiate the unexplained assortment of locks and receive the parcel from the delivery driver within the eight-second window they give you. If you don't manage this, a card will come through the door saying 'We attempted to deliver your parcel but you were out, so hard cheese to you,' and then your host might be left without any insulin.

It is still possible for consternation-causing incidents to occur when taking a shower on empty premises. These days, when taking a shower while alone in someone else's house, I am minded to be just as prudent with my dress code to and from the shower as I would be if everyone were at home. If you have said your goodbyes the night before, there is still a very tiny chance that your host's plans have changed and they are still on the premises. Even if you know for a fact that your host has vacated, there is the spontaneous wild card of an undiscussed keyholder materializing at any time.

The French bedspring testers left me alone in the apartment after their night of bouncy mineral-water-fuelled experimentation, using what little energy they must have had left to drag themselves to their day jobs early in the morning. When a more palatable hour came around, I helped myself to a shower. Abandoning all the hallway etiquette to which I had adhered on the days that my host had been at home, I waltzed back from the bathroom wearing nothing but a slightly inadequately fitting towel. I dared to believe that there would be no issue with this on empty premises. This was an unfortunate assumption on my part because, when I threw open the bathroom door to perform my carefree catwalk strut, it was to the sight of the female bedspring tester's Herculean father wielding a plunger. The towel was so alarmed by the intrusion into our privacy that it passed out, falling wholly and at once to the floor. I attempted to reinstate it but my dignity was unsalvageable.

Monsieur Plunger and I both perceived each other as illegitimate entities. The playing field was pitifully uneven. He had a large dog. I had some shampoo. He was fully dressed. I was wearing a very small portion of the towel, which amounted to little more than a flannel over my gentleman's area. His expression of consternation was low-pitched and fear-inducing. Mine was a shrill descant over his thundering bass melody, making it plain that

I was unlikely to triumph if the confused fracas were to esculate to a degree of combat beyond that of good-natured verbal discussion.

Somehow, we patched things up. I was able to summon the French vocabulary with which to explain myself and the plunger handle managed not to find itself rammed up my person, in contradiction to what I suspect had been the gentleman's instinctive Plan A. He went about his plumbing while I sheepishly went to get dressed. 'I wish she'd told me!' he chortled in French, with the characteristic understatement of the party whose genitalia hasn't just been exposed. I rather wished the same, and I suspect with a greater intensity of feeling than him. People who end up in such compromising situations have usually had a more sensual time than is to be afforded by a solo night on the sofa.

You might wish to present your host with a gift to express your appreciation for their hospitality. If you have not already given your gift, you could leave it somewhere prominent so that your host will be reminded upon their return that you are a decent and thoughtful person and probably didn't mean to activate the burglar alarm at 4 AM. I have scored many a tactful bulls-eye with my thank offerings over the years: chocolates for hosts who turned out to be diabetic, flowers for those suffering from acute hay fever, that type of thing. Donating a kitten to distract from the absence of the one you couldn't talk out of jumping out of the bedroom window could be an appropriate and thoughtful token.

On departure in solitary circumstances, you will be responsible for locking up the house for as many hours as your host will be gone before they arrive back to a home that is starkly empty of your scintillating personality. It is up to you to ensure that the property is secure and that the interior is as unblemished as it was when you arrived, or at least when your host left. A fairly standard procedure is that you lock up on departure with a key that your host has left with you, dropping it through the letterbox when you have done so. This isn't too difficult to get wrong.

An alternative to being left with a key is being told that 'the door will lock behind you,' and therefore 'just' to 'pull the door closed when you leave'. This theoretically foolproof approach rids you of any ambiguity as to whether you locked the door properly and stops you from accidentally going home with the key. However, it brings with it a disconcerting finality. The moment you hear the confirmatory click from the Yale lock and the solid report of the wood meeting the frame is the same moment at which you will remember that you've left your car keys, wallet or maybe even that pesky gorilla carelessly discarded inside the house. There is no way back. Well, certainly no way back that doesn't involve a sledgehammer and you probably haven't thought to bring one. Actually, I hope you haven't.

If you're feeling particularly sentimental, you can look through the letterbox and perhaps get a teasing glimpse of your essential yet abandoned object smiling back at you. You might even be able to put your arm through the door and try to grab the item if it appears to be within reach, after which you may pass some fraught minutes attempting to retract your limb from the letterbox. If your arm proves to be irreversibly wedged and it was your phone that you overlooked to carry out of the house with you, you will have to wait for a concerned and obliging neighbour to appear and agree to call the fire brigade to free you because, for obvious reasons, you won't be able to call them yourself.

Leaving things behind is a critical problem if they're items fundamental to your journey, such as train tickets or the aforementioned car keys. If it's only your knickers, it's merely awkward. You might not have left anything behind at all, but the fastening of the door will also coincide with your realising that you left a window open or didn't turn the gas fire off. At the very least, it will prompt you to think twice about something along those lines, rendering you an increasingly nervous wreck as the rest of your day unfolds.

Whether you're leaving under your own auspices or being seen off from the front door with a lavish display of adulation, it is important to give a moment's thought to the retrieval of outerwear and other accessories. If you are leaving under different weather conditions from those that prevailed on your arrival, you will likely depart without the coat, scarf and umbrella with which you arrived. My grandfather used to manage to leave a flat cap hanging up in every house he visited, ensuring that everyone upon whom he called was left with a tangible reminder of the occasion. One can only assume that his return journeys were characterised by a cold head, although seemingly not one of such severity that it ever registered with him. Several other elderly relatives of mine would frequently go home and forget the walking sticks with which they'd arrived, calling to mind the story of the faith healing session that had been so unsatisfactory that even the man in the wheelchair had got up and walked out.

It is more complex if you're staying with someone who hospitably greeted you on arrival with the words 'Shall I take your coat?' Handing over my coat when arriving at someone's house often feels like I am putting down a security deposit. My coat and the contents of its pockets will be returned to me, ideally but not necessarily with the accompanying scarf, if I manage to conduct myself in a seemly manner throughout my stay and don't damage any valuable ceramics or say 'bollocks' in front of puritanical family members. Of course, I realise that this is not really the motive behind the gesture but perhaps it is actually something that hosts with standards to enforce should consider.

I always engage in a moment's frantic harvesting of everything my coat contains that I might need during my stay before handing the garment over, after which the host conveys it to a secret location in a remote wing of the house. If the host is still at home when I'm leaving, this coat-storage arrangement tends to be to my advantage because there's more chance of someone else remembering that I need to take my coat away than there is of me doing the same. However, if you've been left to let yourself out and your host has placed your coat and thus your wallet and keys in, for all you know, a vault hundreds of metres underground to which only they have the access code, you could be a bit screwed.

If I leave the house after my host, I always feel the need to draw a line under the visit by sending them a cheery text message to report that I've successfully vacated, that I've done whatever they asked me to do with the key, that I don't think I've ruined the house or caused suffering to any pets and to say what a joy it was to see them and how thoroughly grateful I am for their generous and congenial hospitality. I always feel a modicum of relief upon receiving a response to this message, ideally one built around a theme of it having been at least average to have spent time with me and that it might not be a complete chore for us to meet again at some point.

If, now that the normal level of distance has been resumed and someone who is usually responsive doesn't answer your plenary tying-up of loose ends, it could simply be that they are still grafting their fingers to the bone in the office. However, if they haven't responded by the end of the day, their house now being palpably empty as a result of your absence, you might experience a niggling sensation that you could have done something wrong. Has the house caught fire as a result of your forgetting to switch something off and is your host therefore too busy fighting the flames to tell you what a pleasure your company was? Has some money or other property gone missing and they think you've swiped it? Are they allergic to the gift you left on the table and was your gesture therefore misconstrued as an assassination attempt? Did you miss the bin when cutting your toenails? Did you forget to flush the toilet before leaving?

Sometimes, of course, there's a natural break in communication for a little while after a visit. This can even be with people with whom you're usually in regular contact, as you both unwind from the atypical proximity of sleeping under the same roof. All the same, it's nice to have some sort of confirmation that your visit hasn't put them off ever seeing you again.

If your host is at home until the moment of your departure, you will be spared your ride through this galaxy of irrational hypotheses. Stepping – or being pushed – over the threshold and gaily bogging off with everyone's best wishes shouldn't impose too many obstacles. The only way I've ever been known to cramp my style significantly on supervised departure – and this is something worth taking a moment's care over as you compose the moment that will form your hosts' lasting feelings about you until next you meet – has been when leaving people's flats via unlit hallways. You are the person leaving the flat and therefore it is you who has stepped out of the door and therefore it is you, not your host, who will step into unfamiliar and pitch-dark territory and be needing to scrabble about for the light switch. Your host might tell you where the switch is but, before they do that, you will instinctively press the first button you can feel on the wall near the door. I have lost count of the times that I have done this and invoked the services of a doorbell rather than a light.

The first time I managed this was when trying to leave an apartment that contained a sleeping baby. Four adult members of the household were present at the door as I did this and my misjudgement prompted them all – by this point with superfluous retrospect – to shush me in a horrified manner. I'm not sure what they expected me to do to rectify my error. They highlighted to me the cosmic extent to which I was an imbecile and did so with such clarity of tone that their display of outrage was, I felt, creating a bigger disturbance to the baby's slumber than had my innocent mistake.

'The baby's asleep,' one person hissed. There followed in the background the unmistakable screams of an infant in their first seconds of waking.

'No, he's not – listen!' I drolly countered with the weakest and least reciprocated of smiles, before seeing myself out of the building on redundant tiptoes.

The second time I made the equivalent blunder, I somehow managed to engage the doorbell of the flat next door. This triggered a similarly helpful chorus of people to inform me heatedly that I had not turned on the light – as was self-evident by the continuation of darkness –

but rung the neighbour's bell. My blunder was further confirmed by the arrestingly loud gong sound that was to be heard on the other side of the wall when I let go of the switch and by the subsequent materialisation of a slightly irritable middle-aged gentleman in the frame of the next door along, wearing only a tee-shirt that he had clearly misjudged as being long enough to preserve decency. His emanating modesty offered me the comfort of no longer being the only person on the scene to have made a miscalculation. The scene unfolded at around 8:30 AM and the man was apparently not a morning person. He offered some irritated grunts and everybody agreed that I was lamentably simple-minded. In the time since these episodes, I have, despite my best efforts, seen myself off people's premises by resonating a joyful chime or two around their property or by unwittingly summoning a party of bleary-eyed, unacquainted neighbours to throw me an impromptu, ill-tempered and confused farewell party.

A classic conclusion to a visit to someone's house, if you are driving home, is when you get into your car and try to grin your way through the feeling of self-consciousness while your host stands on the doorstep waiting to wave you off, with the front door wide open and the heat freely escaping from the house. They feel equally awkward and don't know where to fix their gaze as you settle into the vehicle and remove the coat that you carefully remembered to retrieve and put on as you left. You might then set the satnav or adjust your mirrors. If you need to do anything before setting off that takes more than twenty seconds, it's probably best to do it once you're around the corner. Your host does not know whether just to shut the door there and then or if it is maybe more affable to see things through until you're on your way. Regardless of how long you take, they will often continue to stand there, smiling and waving until you're completely out of sight because it's the social convention and the convivial thing to do. It also enables them to make sure you've finally fucked off.

Postlude

Benjamin Franklin once hospitably remarked that 'guests, like fish, begin to smell after three days'. We spend the entirety of our time in other people's houses endeavouring not to smell. Usually, the biggest challenge when staying with someone is making it through the first night without emitting any sort of unpleasant odour.

As I have unpacked throughout this book, being an overnight guest can take us across the usual boundary of someone's personal space. We enter into a temporary arrangement with them where our universes collide and cohabit. It is a time when people offer us a glimpse into their private lives and we experience them in their natural habitats. We exist (sometimes accidentally) within sight and sound of their doing things that we normally associate only with people from our own household. Being in such relatively close proximity to someone sleeping can put us on high alert owing to our keenness not to disturb their peace. We also want to keep a tasteful and courteous distance from our hosts' personal procedures while completing our own, getting washed and dressed via a carefully strategized or haphazardly timed sharing of facilities. We don't want our hosts to think badly of us. We want to establish ourselves as slick and unobtrusive and well-brought-up people. Above all, we want to avoid embarrassment.

So many things go on behind closed doors and people incorporate such a wealth of quirks into their daily lives that there will be all sorts of possible predicaments on which I haven't ruminated in these pages. Many of them would undoubtedly be so fantastic as not to have occurred to me, much less to have afflicted me. On the other hand, a great many visits will pass without any incident at all, and many people may wonder what's led me to write a volume of such fanciful hysteria. When I told one of my more strait-laced friends that I was writing this book, he was bemused and said 'I stay with lots of people and nothing ever happens'. I assured him that his time would come. Perhaps I am just a magnet for these absurd domestic happenings and of course, I can hardly be considered to be helping myself when I go carrying people's microwaves down flights of stairs in the middle of the night. Maybe a second publication is required for potential hosts, advising on how they can safeguard their homes, their pets and their peace if I am on the premises.

Only days ago, I wondered whether some of the episodes described in this book had merely been freak occurrences rather than things that the average house guest might need to consider in a risk assessment. I had just been writing up the section about taking a shower when I happened to be doing just that in a house I had never previously visited. I entered the shower with a healthy scepticism of my own hypothesis but the situation merrily proceeded to kick me in the balls. The shower spluttered to life and then pressure-washed me with a piercing chill before opting to boil me instead. When I tried to adjust things, I was left covered in soap as the temperature plummeted to a frightfully cold degree. I briefly reflected that I would have been quite happy in the circumstances to have been proven wrong, and for this book to have been rendered redundant, but I left the bathroom feeling affirmed in my conviction that staying in other people's houses is an expedition of hazards and indiscretions that require permanent vigilance. Surely, it can't just be me for whom this is the case.

Despite the labyrinth of potential catastrophes, staying with people is a wonderful thing. Receiving hospitality is a way of forming deeper connections and spending quality time with your friends and family without needing to worry about the journey home. It is a way of briefly being a part of the everyday life of another person or another place. As I wrote in the foreword, it is a compliment that you've been invited to be there, or at least not forced to leave. Additionally, it offers an escape from your everyday regime while providing more excitement and adventure than going on a safari. Indeed, if you open the wrong door at the wrong time or make a misjudgement with your towel, you might respectively see or exhibit beastly things that could give the African Savanna a run for its money.

I should emphasize, in case this book has created the impression that I am not a safe bet to be untethered in your home, that I do possess a level of introspection that makes me go to great lengths to avoid succumbing to the catalogue of faux pas meditated upon in these chapters. Indeed, it is this hyper-adversity to being a nuisance that has enabled me to make such a comprehensive evaluation of the pitfalls of being a house guest. My blunders are made with the best of intentions. If you catch me crossing the landing with a kitchen appliance, it'll be because I'm trying to avoid waking you up. If your bathroom is under a foot of water after my shower, be assured that I fought both icy and scalding waters in my attempts to curb the floods. I can't promise that I won't end up taking your smalls home but please know that, if I do, it'll be an honest mistake.